LIVING IN AN AGE OF SURVIVAL
VIRAL FRAGMENTS FROM TRUMP TO COVID

JAMES BATCHO

©2022 James Batcho
Seoul, South Korea
www.jimbatcho.com

Published by Glass Spider Publishing
www.glassspiderpublishing.com

ISBN: 979-8-9851773-2-9

Library of Congress Control Number: 2021923839

Cover photo: Bled, Slovenia ©James Batcho

GLASS
SPIDER
PUBLISHING

I am grateful for the unwavering love and support of my wife, Siyun Kim, whose belief in us made for a survival worth living.

CONTENTS

PREFACE

This book was written while I was working on other things. It chronicles a particular period of time: the lead-up to the US presidential election in 2016 through the ongoing anxiety of the pandemic in the summer of 2021. It is a work of philosophical inquiry, but without the discipline of method. Instead it is a series of thought-pieces, some long and others brief, about a volatile and divisive time in the mediation of our political and social lives.

It began as a document I started in 2016. As I was working on my academic research on aesthetics and epistemology,[1] my readings were also affected by the news reports and social media posts I was absorbing at the time. The document functioned as a stream for other thinking. I used it as a holding bin for philosophical ideas that were mostly political but also covered a range of other areas. I hoped that they might someday expand into larger essays or book ideas. Many of them became social media posts intended to provoke discussion.

---

[1] Primarily, I was working on my original concepts of "audibility" and "unseeing." Through 2017, I was completing a manuscript that became *Terrence Malick's Unseeing Cinema* (Palgrave-Macmillan, 2018), about the connections of hearing, listening, memory and spirit in film. This work continued into a second, still uncompleted, book on audible epistemology. Essays completed from 2018-2021 centered on concepts of audibility in film theory, and philosophic works on pre-Socratic, Hellenistic and early Christian concepts of aesthetics and epistemology.

Sometime in early 2021, I realized that these fragmented idea-sketches had become a whole. The chronology of events marked a period of change and the document was chronicling this change. In 2016, Trump was elected. Through the horrors of his presidency, liberalism attempted to respond to his political rupture. We promised resistance. From him, key shifts in the discourses over rights for women and people of color emerged, but our strategies of thinking and communicating became mired in mediated demands. Resistance died. Then came Covid, with all the despair, anxiety and unrest it brought, and a rapid turn toward compliance to universal morality. Trumpism after Trump retained its dialectical core. Inquiry, resistance and creative skepticism were dying. This liberal descent into opposition and conformity, these five years of development, became the book.

Each thought expressed is the thought of that one day, that one moment in time. As events change, my views on things change. I am a United States citizen who, during this time, was living primarily in Asia. In 2016 and 2018, I survived a pair of health crises. From this, I developed a profoundly different relationship with my body. In early 2020, as the pandemic emerged, I was living in Taiwan. I was protected from the lockdowns, protests and social unrest that my friends and family in the USA and Europe faced. I "participated" in these events only through screens. In Taiwan, I was going through a different struggle from what was happening outside. I was separated, by State and/or workplace mandate—I was never quite sure as there were no documented rules or laws—from the person I love most. I said goodbye to her in February, 2020, planning to reunite about six weeks later; I came through immigration hours before the travel corridors were cut off. I did not see her again until January, 2021 for a five-week period. (To get this trip approved by my employer, it had to be pitched as an agreement to marry, but that's another story.) During our year apart, the relationship survived through screens with the promise of a return to someday, perhaps, being *lived*.

These personal aspects have undoubtedly affected my political attitude, as I aimed to philosophically work through what was unfolding through my screens. Scanning through my personal, aggregated "knowledge streams" of Facebook moralism and Google News imperatives, I digested a particular version of liberal centrism. Meanwhile, deeply reading texts by Nietzsche, Deleuze, James, Beauvoir, Arendt, Han and others nurtured me with a radical, creative antagonism. In this mixture, I found my politics shifting. I watched our liberal strategies either fail terribly or mutate into an increasing acceptance of the logic of conformity, correction and control. As the pandemic grew, so did my sense of unease and urgency. Writing became cathartic, and as time passed, my frequency of entries increased.

The book ends at the end of August 2021, still in the midst of the pandemic, but reunited with my wife. When it came time to complete the book, I only made minor changes to the writing that happened. I wanted to keep the spirit of spontaneity intact with all its flaws. And there are many flaws: bad predictions, faulty conclusions, poor argumentation, nascent readings of philosophical texts. As a fragmentary work, there is no thesis to restate and defend, but there are ideas to draw from it. In the development of the writing, a constellation formed, a worldview that values living in an age that demands survival. It is a book of rebellion in a time of compliance, one that aims toward the future.

These fragments are arranged the same as their original chronological date. In that document, I also wrote a timestamp (say, 19:35). On some days, I wrote more than one fragment. For this book, I've deleted all time indications. If there were two fragments for the same day, I've replaced the timestamp with asterisks (*****) to separate one thought from the later one.

FRAGMENTS 1: 2016

2 May, Walnut Creek

I wonder if our writing inclinations are aligned with our amorous strategies... the way we seek (or hope to find) love. One approach is to write as if one is going to engage in some social environment—a singles bar, an after-class coffee get-together with fellow classmates. Here one reaches out to the group to find one's reader, *that* reader, which is one way to find love (and one way to write). The other inclination, the more romantic one, is to be less social, antisocial even, to write me with the hope that someone, the right one, will eventually find me. Intention versus waiting: I write intending to find readership or I write waiting for my reader to find me.

8 June, Chiang Mai

Is is metaphysics. But *is* is not working for me these days. *And* is where the fun is. *And* is crazy metaphysics. *And* is the between of things and thoughts. I like *and*. *Or* is another flight altogether. I can't even deal with *or* right now.

10 June, Chiang Mai

The things that we truly love are the things that we loved before we knew who we were, before the super-ego began its regular assault on the ego. Everything that I love now—cinema, travel, philosophy, writing and reading, landscape, situating myself in a certain place at a certain time—all stems from my love of music. All other loves came out of that one great love, the one who is always with me and will never leave me. The *ideal* love that can only express in its *actuality*.

20 June, Chiang Mai

It has taken me some time in all the philosophy I've been reading to come to the realization that one cannot read a work of philosophy without knowing whom its author is responding to. Nietzsche is perhaps the most tragic of all, as he left behind a series of disappointments: once so in love with Socrates before he broke his heart, so in love with Schopenhauer before he broke his heart, so in love with Wagner before he broke his heart. Nietzsche's literature is an impassioned series of heartbreaks.

5 September, Walnut Creek

The question asked now is "why HRC and Trump?"[2] Why these two unlikable candidates? This question cannot be asked as if they are independent of the world through which we have come to know them. "The media," is not something *else*; it is the garden in which they sprouted. Neither HRC nor Trump exists without this essence.

What a glorious bounty "the media" has reaped from this. She, the middle ground, consensus-building, corporately-funded, condescending rationalist that corporate media ideology is grounded upon—a mirror to project the appearance of reasoned objectivity which maintains its product. He, the headline-making, hate-inspiring, anti-rationalist, shock-that-must-be-told, narrative butterscotch that assures that people will tune in to see what he's going to say next so that we can sell another few tubes of Colgate to fight the cavities. It's perfect for capitalist media, an immaculately conceived, money-making machine.

In the midst of this is *we*, the public, like fish in water, unaware of the presence of water. We swim eternally in a sea of media, oxygenated by money and ideology. But we believe we move in a sea nurtured by facts, from which we can cast a reasonable vote. This sea is not a sea of otherness. We made this sea that we cannot see. We live in it, soak in it as we consume it; we love it, love to hate it, hate to love it. We try to bring it closer, this slathering sea of ourselves; we feel the endless wash of this corporate ocean that we all willingly drown ourselves in.

After this election is over, I hope the question "why HRC and Trump?" will be answered: because we love our corporate media that

---

[2] Hillary Rodham Clinton and Donald J. Trump, the two candidates running for US president in 2016.

we make through our consumption. They are us, our gills and fins, our thinking, our very consciousness. There is no distance; we are all soaking in it. We do not merely watch; we pay with our attention. We absorb and become. The essence is us, we the essence. Trump and HRC, the leaders of our times, the products of our clouded participation.

But perhaps... perhaps there is a little sunlight above the water if we choose to look upward at the surface. Perhaps, after this election is over, we can stop swimming and just let our bodies float upward to the void. But we'd have to first admit that we are the gilled beast. It is up to us to drain the blood from the beast that is oneself. Let the blood drain to the bottom, as our carcass floats upward to be reborn in transcendence. Perhaps, if we do this—through one *I-don't-give-a-fuck* at a time—we can bleed it as we bleed ourselves, drain corporate media from the *us* that is *it*. Don't give it another sight or listen. Just stop swimming. See how any of this water lives without its source of nourishment as we drift upward, slowly, eyes closed, ignorant, immobile and undeterred. It is possible.

19 September, Walnut Creek

As I read Spinoza's Ethics, *my third time through...*

If we think of the media lifeworld not as something separate from us, not as an object which we can distance and then rationalize, but more of a univocal substance through whose attributes we are always already within the state of rationalizing, then the media becomes the God within ourselves that we do not pray to but within which we pray. Our prayers are what we contribute to the lifeworld and receive from it, maintaining our own devotion to what we think we know and nurturing within ourselves the comfort of knowing: a cycling of the same.

And along comes the orange-headed monster, the Devil, interrupting the narrative, the known, the same, by injecting absurdity, abject difference, and a whole lot of *how-is-this-happening* that invites us to freak out or to recognize the absurdity within ourselves. Is this a moment to transform?

20 September, Walnut Creek

When we are young children, growing into adults, we are told to avoid drugs, that they will not solve our problems.

When we are old adults, growing into children, we are told to take drugs, that they will solve our problems.

12 October, Walnut Creek

The need for physical contact is deeply embedded in the psyche and the body. It's the animal in the human who needs this connection with other human animals, composing a different understanding.

Exchanges through current technology have none of this. All these convenient attempts to overcome distances born of loneliness, have no soul, no energy, no sensation. They are perfectly rendered data streams that land in abstract understandings. From these exchanges, we carry away various objects of a stridently mimetic *ethos*: text, images, representations of representations. Social media and screened living is not a connection, it's a constant reminder of the distance, a reminder of the absence of soul, energy, resonance... the closure that distances. This economy, the one nurtured by Clinton-Bush-Obama-Clinton, provides an artificial life, one that preserves and carries the necessary information, a simulacrum of care and friendship. It is not the world we live in; but it is increasingly replacing the idea of living. This life goes straight to the informational center of the mind.

This is why Trump is of little concern to me. I resist this life to remain in the world of the living. Each instance of his representation, each event, is just another understandable, identifiable point which I'm told to care for, attend to, data that I must consider rationally. People today call this privilege, that I am safe from the effects of all these data points of words and comments. This is true. Yet it is also true that this information is nurtured by our attention to it. We nurture Trump by massaging and watering and giving sunlight to all of his little globes of hatred that reproduce themselves thanks to us. Nothing he says would be heard (nor even said) if he did not have us to look at them, listen to them, attend to them, *care* for them.

13 October, Walnut Creek

As the election draws closer, and as I'm instructed socially to feel guilt for choosing to support neither candidate, I'm drawn to Malcolm X.

"I said I felt that as far as the American black man was concerned they were both just about the same. I felt that it was for the black man only a question of Johnson, the fox, or Goldwater, the wolf. ... With these choices, I felt that the American black man only needed to choose which one to be eaten by, the 'liberal' fox or the 'conservative' wolf—because both of them would eat him."

"I didn't go for Goldwater any more than for Johnson— except that in a wolf's den, I'd always known exactly where I stood; I'd watch the dangerous wolf closer than I would the smooth, sly fox. The wolf's very growling would keep me alert and fighting him to survive, whereas I *might* be lulled and fooled by the tricky fox."

"Goldwater as a man, I respected for speaking out his true convictions—something rarely done in politics today. He wasn't whispering to racists and smiling at integrationists. I felt Goldwater wouldn't have risked his unpopular stand without conviction. He flatly told black men he wasn't for them—and there is this to consider: always, the black people have advanced further when they have seen they had to rise up against a system that they clearly saw was outright against them. Under the steady lullabies sung by foxy liberals, the Northern Negro became a beggar. But the Southern Negro, facing the honestly snarling white man, rose up to battle that white man for his freedom—long before it happened in the North."

- The Autobiography of Malcolm X[3]

We are not the same but I feel the words. I know what it means to see the society that implores me to conform from the *outside*, feeling a passion of resistance, driven by a different imperative.

---

[3] 1965, Ballantine Books.

14 October, Walnut Creek

David Fincher's *Alien 3* gets a bad rap, but I always loved it. He ripped away the comfortable family ending of James Cameron's *Aliens* and brought it back to her battle against the hyper-masculinity of the phallic alien face by doubling down, placing her in a hyper-masculine prison camp. In the end, the masculine emerges in a character previously redeemed as a nurturing ally, the one who saved her: Bishop is now in human, not android, form. He appears as the State, as spokesman for the technocratic, militaristic power structure, her last hope for personal survival.

And she, forced against the wall, with this technology and ideology literally impregnated within her, decides to take the only act of free will she can. She kills both herself and the weapon, ending the object of this masculine agenda. Her death is both Greek and Christian—tragic yet somehow transcendent.

22 October, Walnut Creek

The thing that science fiction does so well is to play out two lines of action that respond to each other. Good scriptwriting accomplishes this anyway, but sci-fi does it particularly well because of the unique structural elements of the genre. We think of sci-fi in terms of *space*, outer space; but it is also about the space of the idea, the idea that gives itself space as an ethics. Externally, we have the material situation; internally, we have the psychological idea.

Blade Runner proposes that in the future there is a material divide between Los Angeles and the Off-world Colonies. This is a spatial divide—the immanent dystopia and the transcendent salvation. The economics and biogenetics of privilege lie at the core of the possibility of transcendence. (*Gattaca* traces the same themes, but in reverse—the biologically engineered are the masters, not the slaves.) The privileged will always be able to occupy the space of privilege and the possibility of transcendence. So it's a spatial matter —not this "place" but the other. There are many other examples of this in literature and even in political theory. The divisions, sometimes rendered metaphorically, of something to leave behind and something else that we recognize (that we see) and aim to attain.

While this division is acted out in the space of material events, a version of it plays out in the mind. A character internalizes the division as a dialectic played out in the psyche. This struggle becomes a choice of whether to fight against or accept what is given materially (consider Cypher in *The Matrix*). Through the actions of characters, an ethics forms. The hero is the one who comes to resist the grand scientific plan of power and domination and becomes a revolutionary. Each developing thought, idea and action builds the architecture of resistance.

Applied to today's politics and the possibilities of *resistance*, the battle isn't played out as force against force, the haves versus have-nots, nor an acceptance of the world of *there* as a utopia or the world of *here* as dystopia. The future of now that the past created is flattened out, good enough. Instead, what we say and do and think— primarily at the economic, consumerist and social levels—renders activity as merely an idea, a virtue to "post." The dialectic is internalized and passive, the dystopian and utopian within us are always present at the same time, and our ethical acts happen at the level of approvals and rejections, likes and dislikes. Life is not an allegory. Today it defies cinematic action. Politics disappears into the psyche.

29 October, Walnut Creek

The only reason to speak is because it is unsayable.

This thought came to mind while thinking about Ludwig Wittgenstein, in whom I'm now immersed for an essay I'm co-writing. To speak is not to state what *is*, but rather an act of stating what cannot be known, otherwise there would be no reason to speak about it. The reason I express something to another person in language is because we have not yet reached an agreement, and therefore one of us has the need to say something.

For Wittgenstein, Bertrand Russell's problem was he was trying to say something that had to be shown. Regarding the "picture theory," if you think of a person and a picture of a person, the picture must have something in common that connects them in order for it to be a picture of that person.

> "Now, Wittgenstein's claim was that you can't picture what a picture has to have in common. So a proposition can picture a fact, but a proposition can't picture the pictorial relationship. That has to be shown."
>
> - Ray Monk[4]

In other words, you can't say the *relation*. It has to be shown rather than said. "The similarity isn't a thing that you see."

This is why relations are so key to the work I'm doing on epistemology, aesthetics and ethics. A relation is unsayable in fact or in logic. It has to be expressed in some other way.

---

[4] *Ludwig Wittgenstein: The Duty of Genius* (1991, Vintage Books).

9 November, Walnut Creek

I suppose what comes next is the blame. Which category of American is to blame for this election result? We will place boxes around low-income whites. Yes, this is true. But we must also blame high-income whites, the elite class, including those who elevated Clinton into position. Perhaps then what we're witnessing is trickle-down rationality—the idea that the elite will lead from the top and filter down to everyone below. What we forgot is that this 99%/1% thing is not a joke. We forgot that people are more aware of their own worlds than we think, that the concern of so many is how the system is rigged. Democrats forget this. The working class lost Bernie and went to Trump, along with an indefinable array of hateful and discontented individuals—an unallied alliance of the powerful and the impoverished.

This is a Democratic Party failure, a media failure, a technocratic, neoliberalist failure. Now, let's own up to that. Let's start making some noise, write some stories, tap into our inner Dionysus and reformulate our images and appearances from the ground up. This doesn't have to be chaos and despair. It's an existential opening.

10 November, Walnut Creek

Count me in as still shocked. Several of my friends predicted a Trump victory but I did not. I thought we'd be here thinking in a different set of realities, about a different kind of fight, another set of conversations that we'd need to have. But this, the racist undertones that cannot be ignored, the fact that I am a white male, that white privilege is now an amplified concept that can't be thought of in only conceptual terms anymore. And I write "anymore" because that might be the case for so many white people but not those for whom this has never been merely a concept. I'm not sure how to write about that yet. But before I leave this alone for now, I have to get down three aspects of this election that have occupied my mind since it unfolded: voting, appearances and values, and ways of thinking. I'm trying not to defend in the form of conclusions, but to inquire, even if I feel in a rather declarative mood today. These to me are philosophical matters, with an emphasis on inconceivability.

      1. <u>Voting/Non-voting</u>. Voting is a right not a mandate. One is free to vote or not vote. But the language that I find people using against those who don't vote has eerie similarities to Christian zealots who cannot conceive of someone not attending church on Sunday. The connection is not merely of attitude. Voting is an act of faith, a prayer. Mathematically, a vote is quite literally insignificant; its significance lies in the individual who engages in an expression of faith—a prayer. And in this, a vote is real and powerful. Voting is the activation of a "vow," as the etymology suggests. To make a vow is to act in faith along one's belief. People who have faith in the system and believe in the candidate make the vow. Fantastic. But you can't expect people to show devotion to something and someone they don't believe in. For those who do not have faith, no amount of shaming and proselytizing is going to change that. My position has always been that people should listen to their conscience, and if they do not believe, we should not expect them to make the vow. What is completely backward is the statement "If you didn't vote you can't complain." If you vote, you have continued the dogma that non-voters find inconceivable. If anyone has a right to complain, it's the people who don't donate to the church. Voting exists as its own container, and those who vote maintain that container. But it is not the entirety of experience nor is it the only means of democratic participation. If people only vote, then the act is a lazy one—the

casting of the vow as a means of absolving the individual from further responsibility.

2. <u>Appearances and values</u>. In philosophical terms, "appearances" is something like *the real phenomena of experience,* beyond which there may also be something extra-real. In media theory, it is what appears on screen and *how it represents* something ostensibly real. The connection and distinction of representation and reality are key to both definitions. Our technological time of the present is constantly both fragmenting and reorganizing this state of division. The media functions primarily in a fragmented state of appearances. Values, by contrast, transcend appearances. They are taken as something unmistakably real. What I wonder is if Trump's success is, in part at least, because people are tuning out appearances —distrustful as so many are of media—and holding onto immutable values. When it comes down to something actionable, his supporters are primarily concerned with core values—jobs, taxation, trade policy. Perhaps then, they were more interested in the some*thing* than the someone. They are less concerned with the language of racism and sexism. While this should alarm us, we should also remember that these particular appearances, his appearances, very real as they are, come to us solely through the fragmented and managed structures of media. Some people (say, white men who interact with other white men) find an *irreality* to these appearances, so the mediated representation has no referent and no effect. There is nothing real *for them*. In addition to the racism of hatred in some, then, is this other racism of ignorance. It is something they already have within themselves every day. There is no appearance, no phenomena, no event—nothing shocking. For them, the mediated versions are a kind of abstraction, existentially muted and distanced, ideological and manufactured, coming from a for-profit industry. Women and people of color, however, deal with these appearances every day—are confronted with them every day—so the mediated representation means everything rather than nothing. It's a direct correlation to

interpersonal experience, a constant reminder of what is abhorrent. But in Trumpworld, this distance from such interpersonal appearances, coupled with (to his supporters) a tiresome repetition of mediated appearances, fades in contrast to values that are as unchangeable as God.

3. <u>There is no one way of thinking</u>. As I sit here presuming how people think, I admit my own folly here—no one can be reduced to A or B. Both Democrats and Republicans seem awash in appearances, in talking to themselves and reifying, through sameness, a likeness of thinking. But I'm going to take the leap and suggest that because the news is dominated by liberal coverage, Trump supporters are more likely to actively discount appearances. Democrats, meanwhile, tend to discount fixed values while talking mostly in mediated appearances. And if values are deeply rooted in faith, appearances are phenomena of experience that traverse along mediated processes of science, streams of information, ephemeral events that gather and contextualize opinion. My liberal friends tend to talk primarily about appearances emerging from and swirling around both candidates—character traits, language, events, lawsuits, ridiculousness belonging to and coming from *the candidate*. This phenomenological mereology is in line with logical, rational thinking. The language *of Trump* is abhorrent, and this is why we discuss it. Trump *himself* is also abhorrent, and for the most hateful, the personification of horror is the identity and the appearance to rally behind. But if my above metaphor applies, that voting is an act of faith, perhaps for some faith comes from another aspect of oneself, something that transcends the candidate. For them, values stand alone, *sui generis*, despite appearances and even party divisions. These are different ways of thinking, but even as I'm placing things in two categories, what we actually have are only tendencies. Thought is individual, generative, and the forces built up from thought tend to gather and become "understood" along pre-existing lines (prior appearances and prior values). If there is a positive to take amid the

horror of Trump it is that creative thought is now more available to us than ever. Breaking the Clinton behemoth was a good thing. I already see necessary changes taking place away from prior lines of thought. So I think this is a time for creativity in thinking, not only in realizations of mistakes and an openness to new ideas, but recombinations, pathways that don't yet exist, getting outside of appearances and, as with Nietzsche, re-valuating our values.

The news media does not do values, it does appearances, and very poor representations at that. A person's values are already within her/him, while media focuses on various phenomena—statements, lawsuits, scandals, facts—as if this data is somehow going to shift the ground of deep-seated values. We as media consumers and content producers work more with appearances than values, and we express our shock and horror within its ceaseless stream. But amidst it all, values reside unstated within the statement, somewhere more essential.

Values are ineffable, at least regarding socially mediated discourses. Appearances *refer to* values only indirectly. But at the core are practices of dialectical negation. Trump's appearances refer to values he negates—equal rights, decency, logic, reason, common sense, universalism, utility. In this he is *different*; his strategy of negation is shocking to Democrats and other centrists. Clinton's appearances refer to what they've always been; and so these appearances are the *same*—the same language, the same mannerisms, the same logic, the same decency, the same performance. They all conform to the familiar strategies and practices of common media narratives. In other words: Trump's appearances *appear as new* and cannot be ignored; Clinton's appearances appear as the same and are ignorable or easily dismissible. Because Trump's appearances are new, they dominate. Clinton's *essence* may be different (she is a woman) and this probably only adds to the misogynistic rejection of her essence and her values; at the same time her *appearances* are the same, and people today are tired of being exploited by the same.

The critical element of *belief* is fully evident in this relation between appearance-based knowledge, consumption and production, and the values underlying and transcending them. Again, at the risk of generalization, one can say that a Democratic voter is probably more likely to believe in the idea of science, which in its mediated representation is relational to how things appear; a Republican voter is more likely to believe in the idea of God, independent of empirical evidence and appearances. Pragmatically, a Democrat may be voting from an *a posteriori* standpoint, and a Republican from an *a priori* one, even if not consciously acknowledged. Values are internalized as independent, absolute, normative (Republican) or dependent, referential, mutable (Democrat).

I am not going to risk assuming what any voter is voting for and against. But I'll throw out the notion that as we will, in the coming months, attempt to contain and define why a Trump voter makes the leap toward him, perhaps there is this as one of the reasons easily discarded: these cultural aspects, manifest as mediated appearances, are not votable to many. The appearance of abstract notions of justice, sympathy and equality are not local enough to elicit *care*. We cannot forget the element of hate, which is real. At the same time, maybe *some* Trump supporters are smarter than we give them credit for because they do tune out the appearances that are delivered through a political-media structure that depends on such appearances to maintain its wealth and power. Maybe. Regardless, I do feel that casting people aside as ignorant doesn't help us to understand each other. If we continue to do this we risk exacerbating rather than eliminating the sexism and racism that we find so evident and yet so elusive. This is how appearances work, as Heidegger reminds us: as they show, they hide.

17 November, Chiang Mai

The thing that I fear is the repetition of sameness in thinking, a strident and ongoing opposition of conservative vs liberal. If this election has taught us anything it's that *thought*—in the sense of a zeitgeist of thinking—had become ossified, enclosed around fixed forms. I'm mostly targeting progressive thinking that had over the past couple of decades stopped progressing and instead—for convenience perhaps, for economics most certainly—accepted the influx of neoliberal and technocratic advances.

This is why philosophy to me is extremely important in this era of Trump. Politics, economics and science deal in dualities, patterns, containers and objects. Their methods of change tend to be oppositional and reactive within the conventions that have been perfected and reproduced. Philosophy, at its best, is a history of responsive change in thinking, of *developments of thinking*. The thought of this age is not philosophical, it is not showing a willingness to develop and change. Like the histories of politics and nations, sometimes a rupture invites an opportunity for a shift. This needs to be the time of a shift forward rather than an entrenchment. I see many people talking of the injustice of the election, but it seems this was a fair election. They speak of a need to consolidate power around the prior/existing structures of contemporary liberalism. This means people are not accepting *why* Trump occurred, which was a fragmentation of the liberal elite. I believe that if Bernie Sanders was our choice, the rupture would have been positive, and I fear that with Trump the rupture is grounded in negativity and extremism. But Zizek is right, as much as we are resistant to admitting it: there is an open invitation here to respond. It's just that we can't see it yet.

If philosophy is the history of thinking, then this is the time to give ourselves an era. In doing some research today I came across some interesting words by one of my favorite thinkers, Henri Bergson.

He's usually found in discussions of memory and time, but his resistance to prior conceptual thinking is applicable to this era. His language in today's connotations may seem odd. He advocates a rupture in thinking that is drawn from one's "intuition" and an "intellectual sympathy." Intuition here is not the new age definition, but an attentive self-consciousness *within* the flow of time. In this, thinking doesn't analyze from a safe distance but penetrates into a field of potentiality. Rather than fixity for analysis or closures around ideas, he wants us to draw ourselves into the mobility of the lived world. He admits:

"This is extremely difficult. The mind has to do violence to itself, has to reverse the direction of the operation by which it habitually thinks, has perpetually to revise, or rather to recast, all its categories."[5]

While metaphysics/philosophy is his aim, this is an ethical plea. We must resist our own dogmas that fall into existing systems or representations. It is a positive violence that breaks one into the field of the new.

Perhaps one area in which we can enact such a benevolent violence is in how we obtain information about the events of our world. Currently, fake news is a hot issue. An old way of thinking (classic pragmatism) is to identify a fixed concept ("fake news") and find a practice, legal or otherwise institutional, to eliminate the problem. This would be like identifying a tumor and surgically removing it, ignoring the lifestyle choices that led to the growth. Fake news is a problem. But the bigger problem is *news*. Illegitimate sources often spread lies. But "legitimate" corporate media makes a financial killing by continually spreading self-serving truths, indulging

---

[5] Henri Bergson, *Introduction to Metaphysics* (1999, Hackett).

in Trump stories while advocating for Clinton's candidacy (both aspects contribute to the institution's financial interests).

A wider approach is to find a means of breaking the profit motive in media. Instead of buying a subscription to the NYT or other for-profit companies (as John Oliver suggests), and instead of lazily relying on a Google or other aggregator, do a search for non-profit sources and learn what they're all about. If enough people were more discriminating in their opinion-gathering, we could do violence to the stranglehold of corporate media, which is omnipresent and which is beholden to advertisers, not the public good.

This is one example of countless fields of availability toward enacting change. Change, real change, is not going to come from falling back into the bloated Democratic Party machine. It's going to come from new pathways of thinking, new ideas and new forms. There is an ethics to our participation; a vote is the least impactful form of participation. Change happens through a shift in mindset and a courage that creates excitations of newness.

In the face of the immanent dangers of "sides" that adhere and react to each other, we need an alternative that is not an opposition. This is the time to enter into sympathy with our time. We need to create an era of new thinking.

21 November, Chiang Mai

These comedians I used to admire and enjoy—Jon Stewart, John Oliver, Bill Maher—I don't want to hear from them anymore. All their well-reasoned outrage, set pieces of amusement via paths of shame, the sharable echo-chamber of self-importance, bolstering the reasonable while bracketing out those who do not speak in liberal vocabularies—I no longer have ears for it. This snarky, entertaining theater of exclusion is not for me anymore.

At some point, we're going to have to stop talking about so many leaves and branches, the daily reproduction of shiny evil things. At some point, we're going to have to talk about the soil and the roots, the things we can't see—the discourses that are a little less funny, a little more nourishing. We need to get subterranean, otherwise the whole ecosystem is going to rot through our incessant textual pruning.

28 November, Chiang Mai

Facts are the spirit-pills of atheism.

12 December, Chiang Mai

There are three F-words that I find recycling in various repetitions: "fascism," "facts" and "fake." I'd like to take these words on one by one and suggest that in our attempts to do the right thing, we might be doing a lot of damage to values that we hold dear. (And by "we," I mean progressives, liberals, my people, those who I feel are in danger of doing a disservice to such values.)

Beginning with the deployment of "fascism," *Rolling Stone* for example (there are countless examples, usually clickable rants from famous entertainers) warns us that "if you were to imagine what impending American fascism would look like, you couldn't place the pieces on the board any more neatly than they've been placed in the last year."[6] In the next paragraph writer Jesse Berney asks how far this fascism will go and speculates that the first target might be his own industry. Could Trump "start tossing journalists in jail?"

While I recognize the concern, which is larger than journalists, there are many flaws in such speculation. First, Trump would have to go to extraordinary lengths to see this happen. It would require a total dismantling of the various legal standards that are the foundation of the American system plus the complicity on behalf of the public. Could these things happen? It's unlikely. And this unlikelihood is the real danger in using the word. What happens when he doesn't start publicly shattering the foundations of American jurisprudence? What happens when he does nothing that is fascist and instead just does what is far more likely: doing awful things, awful things to the planet, to civil rights, to human rights and decency? These awful things cannot be named so easily as "fascist." And in our lazy tendency to quickly name things into Category X we've missed the point. The bigger fears are not fascism, but that he will use legal means to gradually alter laws and set new precedents. That's not fascism, that's policy.

This leaves us empty of nouns and grappling with various adjectives. What is the name for this nebulous dismantling? We've jumped out with the F-word and it turned out to not be that. Once we've lost the noun "fascism" we've granted validity to its negation: See, he didn't jail anyone, he's not fascist! And the only thing left, once the fascism tag has been drained of its validity, is normalization. And normalization is the biggest thing to worry about with Trump: acceptance that this is how things are.

The second F-word is "facts." Since liberal atheists have no God as a guiding force in conscious behavior, they place their faith in Science to fill the gap. Science will save us; facts will save us. There

---

6 See https://www.rollingstone.com/politics/politics-features/trumps-presidency-is-shaping-up-to-be-an-american-tragedy-118700/.

are several problems with facts, but the main one is that their methodology discounts the conditions under which facts are produced materially and in how prior belief produces them psychologically. We cannot account for the vagaries and infinite swirl of human behavior and thought that gives rise to any fact, nor can we isolate objects of data for study. Facts are not the beginning of knowledge. They're the result of conditions that give rise to their appearance as phenomena. And as any philosopher or psychologist will tell you, what is apparent is not the extent of what is real. Facts deny the unconscious and the unseen and they tend to mask over the resonances that permeate any individual fact that emerges. Deployed politically, facts become weaponized to affirm the existing belief.

This brings us to our third F-word: "fake." Liberals are latching onto this word to battle what is a very real and dangerous problem: that beliefs are formed by inaccurate statements of events. As Heidegger writes in his book on logic, it is an Aristotelian *logos* disconnect, where the statement doesn't accord to the truth. The desire here is for legitimacy, which drops us into a faith in corporate media, the safe zone for un-fake facts. We give faith to media because the media is an organizational tool of legitimacy. The problem here is that its legitimacy is not grounded on facts, rather that facts provide the basis to legitimize itself, its own institution. "Objectivity" is the lifeblood of journalism. Without it, the paper, the news channel, the website makes no income and no capital flows through it. Is it any wonder that Hillary Clinton is speaking out against the problem of fake news? If things had gone her way, and only legitimate news did the coverage, the media conglomerates would be able to filter their version of information, a version that is fundamentally tied to advertising income and audience numbers, which serves her interests as a corporate politician.

Why was the media coverage so obsessed with Trump? Ratings and advertising revenue. The head of CBS admitted it.[7] Why was the media coverage so aligned with Clinton? Why didn't I hear about Bernie Sanders' ideas on CNN or MSNBC? Why didn't I hear about Standing Rock and the Dakota Access Pipeline on CNN or MSNBC? Demographics and a managing of consensus. Neither of the latter two events generated wealth for the broadcaster, so the facts were suppressed in favor of facts about Trump. I know, I watched the news. But had I only watched legitimate news, I wouldn't have become aware of Sanders' platform or learned about Standing Rock. This came from Facebook links to what are now, in many cases, considered fake news outlets. Both were real events, but their facts were not entertaining enough.

Taking all of this together, we have to remember that it is not facts but the conditions-of-fact-generation that is the ground of whatever we might consider fascist or fake or factual in the arena of public opinion.

There is history to our devotion to such profanities. We can look to the 1920s debates between Walter Lippmann and John Dewey, both giants in the formation of American social and political thinking, to gain some sense of precedence. It is well worth reading both Lippmann's *Public Opinion* and Dewey's *The Public and Its Problems* in full.[8] Lippmann is the better known of the two in this particular battle, and indeed he's considered the victor in the media world, a kind of Ayn Rand for news corporations.

Lippmann quite rationally argued that the public could not be trusted to be active democratic participants.

---

[7] See https://www.hollywoodreporter.com/news/general-news/leslie-moonves-donald-trump-may-871464/.

[8] I wrote about this in my master's thesis. I recommend both books, plus John Durham Peters' essay titled "Democracy and American Mass Communication Theory: Dewey, Lippmann, Lazarsfeld." Peters' essay can be retrieved here: https://sites.psu.edu/cas100hvicarosp15/wp-content/uploads/sites/21612/2015/01/JDWLPFL.pdf.

"In his view, the most feasible alternative to such democracy consisted of a technocracy in which government leaders are guided by experts whose objectives and disinterested knowledge go beyond the narrow views and the parochial self-interests of the average citizens organized in local communities. Lippmann saw advocates of participatory democracy as romantic and nostalgic individuals who idealized the role of the ignorant masses to address public affairs and proposed an unrealistic model for the emerging mass society."

- Daniel Schugurensky[9]

Sound like a particular argument? Perhaps the prevailing liberal notion that legitimate institutions and authoritative fact-generation should temper the chaos of fake ideas? If you like this view, you may be a Lippmannite.

Dewey was also a believer in facts, and for my part I don't entirely subscribe to his counter-argument, but he advocated for a participatory role on the part of the public that goes beyond elections and includes discussion, an evolution of education and a truly free press. He proposed that "policies should remain a public trust which must not be manipulable by private interests."[10] This, Dewey admitted, is difficult. Democracy is messy. And I wonder what he would have thought of Facebook and Twitter, not only as private corporations as the most prevalent means of public deliberation, but that such deliberation is entirely divorced from the living, breathing public he wrote of. It's fair then to question Dewey's faith that the people will do the right thing, but also grant that this is not the public he advocated. This corporately enabled public gave us Clinton and Trump, and Trump won the presidency.

---

[9] This quote is from Schugurensky's essay "1922: Walter Lippmann and John Dewey debate the role of citizens in democracy," which can be retrieved at http://schugurensky.faculty.asu.edu/moments/1922lippdew.html.

[10] Ibid.

A closer look at Dewey's critique offers another view: Our problem is not that people are stupid, it is that the institutions of authority and capitalism have turned us into consumers rather than participants. And this is where doing the right thing is polluted by such conditions. We begin our participation at the television/computer/mobile, end it at the voting booth, then call it a day. This legitimizes existing and corrupt structures, all of which are driven by financial interests. It all streams the same lifeblood of liberal corporatism. We educate our young people to be entrepreneurs, singular heroes. We teach to tests and quantify thought and wonder why we accept the data that flows into our news feed, into our souls. We are passive in our involvement. This passivity is often named as "activism" when one is able to "have one's say," as if anything is changeable through such structures.

I would like to think that Dewey would tell us that being active citizens is not about feeding corporate interests and legitimizing corrupt structures of media and democracy. It comes rather by moving our bodies and minds, twisting them in uncomfortable ways, resisting placid consumption. Movements like Occupy Wall Street and Standing Rock are physical, corporeal activities that require people to sacrifice their bodies. But if we cannot personally do this, we must at least be willing to sacrifice our thoughts, to live differently, consume differently... to give our thoughts over to other pathways and not depend on the gathering of information but to become agitated by other discourses... to create things, not for one's brand but to agitate against branding of all kinds, not to make a name for oneself but to lose oneself.

This will not offer us any more knowledge, but it might just re-territorialize the ground upon which we think. What we live and breathe are not facts but environments, territories, immanent planes. It is out of these conditions—not objects, images or facts but as Dewey's friend William James wrote, the flux of relations—that new thought can grow.

FRAGMENTS 2: 2017

1 February, Chiang Mai

As often occurs in doing philosophy, in this case writing some notes on Kierkegaard, I get distracted and start following an unnecessary path. The word that made me pause was "immediate." I've been reading this in lit as *time*, as the *immediate moment* of time. What jolted me was a realization that philosophically it perhaps more often points to a *lack of mediation*. And yet, now scanning through uses of the term, it seems to be employed cavalierly in philosophy, so much so that I don't even know that the *writer* always knows.

After thinking this over for the past hour, it may be that it is best employed (in other words, how I wish to employ it) as a conjoining of the two. Immediacy then is both the instant and the unreasoned. At least for Kierkegaard, perhaps this is the implication.

This in turn led me to an altogether different path—to wonder if a great problem of contemporary society is the abundance of mediacy and the lack of immediacy, the inability to escape the mediated. In this sense, to be mediated is to be bound to something else that lies between the time of oneself and the time of possible thought and action. How then does one find the duration that allows for immediacy? Is immediacy always a *prior to* mediation, or the experience that exists at some *other*, more resonating level of thought? Can one linger in the duration of immediacy enough to rethink whatever an experience is and what it means, not what it is already (mediated) but precisely the opposite—a kind of relation that constitutes an extended reverie, an experience that needs no understanding, which perhaps can lead to a new understanding.

And as I continue thinking, I think about media, about politics, about how we are trying so damned hard to mediate everything. The Trump-media-commodity machine has thrown so much mediation out there for us to mediate that our mediation circuits go berserk. We think of ourselves as rational creatures, with *reasoning* as the tool to mediate the immediate. This media and its mediation comes in chaotic waves of *simulated* immediacy far outpacing reason. He, the master of media, short-circuits the ability to mediate by creating such streams of mediated immediacy. We citizens of rational-technological mediation have only been trained to mediate via the mechanisms, methods and thinking processes of science, logic, law and reason; we have been improperly schooled in immediacy.

Wouldn't it be nice if we took more opportunities to immediate ourselves, to *unmediate* within our instants and moments, to immediate ourselves immediately? Is it not a skill to foster time as itself rather than information, if we taught each other to enter into or create streams of improvisation? It's good that we can still play music, that we still have conversations. But even these forms of expression are suffering from complex and multiple mediations as automated, mechanized, codified or distanced from the immediate. To become immediate, we would need to grant ourselves permission to be improper, incorrect.

Isn't it also interesting that I do this because I have the time to think? I'm not plugged into a defined circuit; I'm allowed to resonate thinking, which allows me to jump on a new, unplanned, un-programmed circuit. This is the problem of the contemporary scholar, who is only granted the time to get the task done. Academia, a circuit

I'm currently exempt from (that is, jobless), has much in common with every other profession in which one professes to complete the work.

3 May, Zhuhai

The Handmaid's Tale is devastating television, and I'd say as well "important" television in that TV is the big entertainment now and it's a great example of how we all slowly incorporate the logic of oppressive forces. I hope it's getting massive audiences. The violence is horrific. I found the third episode in particular one of the most disturbing hours of TV I've ever seen, less from the physical violence, more in the environment of permissibility in its violence: this world of effacement, dehumanization and de/re-feminization, bodies erased of minds, persons erased of names. Aesthetically I appreciate how the editor lingers on faces to let the pain of what is occurring settle in. The whole thing unfolds with a lot of patience and silence, the process of thinking. It allows its characters to internalize the dizzying progression of its horrors.

But the show also subverts itself. After all the trauma that they endure, that we witness, the show ends with some godawful pop music and/or some voiceover that speaks a pedestrian line like "aw fuck." I'm not sure what the intent is here, that all of this can be boiled down to a series of bad days? As in, here's a pop song and a tidy expletive to show that, well darn it, life sucks. And that yeah, just like you're treated like shit in your daily life so are they. And just like you saying "aw fuck" at the end of your day, so do they. In a way— and I say "in a way" because I haven't decided yet—this cheapens both the narrative experience and the ethics offered. Wouldn't it be better for the narrative to unfold the horror of the unknown possibilities of the future that one faces, rather than attempt to relate to existing horrors of the everyday that one currently lives? One is the work of fiction, the other reflects the individual grievances of social media that we ourselves nurture. Perhaps as a work of *entertainment* it is attempting both. But *as* entertainment, the latter subverts the former.

The series has only just begun, but this is *not* a story about the everyday. It is about a society run by men that violently oppresses women. So this kind of lightness at the end flattens out its necessary anguish, a way of suggesting that women just deal with it and keep living. This is common in post-apocalyptic television—the endurance of suffering. It's a Christian *ethos*. Job walks alongside every hero, as Kierkegaard might say. And this is the show's existentialism. It's not a question of whether to keep on surviving but the imperative that one *must* keep on surviving in the midst of incomprehensible suffering. (I sense as well that there is a capitalist element to this, also unstated: keep shopping.) Survival is never in question for its heroes. Just survive and as you survive, maintain an appearance of dignity and subservience. Entertainment must have a relatability factor that helps gain an audience, projecting that this is a heightened version of what women must deal with every day.

Maybe I'm reading it wrong. Maybe this subversion, the "aw fuck" and the uplifting pop song, is an expression of power and agency, and that surviving is the virtue that sustains. Maybe in their furtive conversations, in their expressions of will, in the intelligence that remains, in the fight that we see in Offred's eyes, maybe this is its virtue, and maybe the song and the "aw fuck" is an expression of this, of the humanity and agency that remains. Or maybe I just really hated the way that the pop song masked the screams of the third episode. I don't know. But to me the show would be better if these horrors were not softened, were not made relatable, were more tragic and less entertaining. Horror lies in the confusion, the incomprehensibility. But what one can identify with is what helps generate a good audience. The pop song as cure.

I've never read Margret Atwood's book, so I don't know how this ends. But I know that if TV has its way, there will be some payoff. It will come when the repetition of suffering risks losing the audience. This is TV's catharsis, to fulfill the fantasies of justice that we do not attain in daily life. In the end, it's all been worth it because one has returned, in the form of justice, the violence that was received.

11 May, Zhuhai

Transcendent is a circle. Transcendental is a line, not a dividing line but one upon which we live and think. And here is the difference between the Buddhists and the Greeks... at least in the sense of the eternal, the infinite. And perhaps I should add: at least in the sense of Buddhism vs Deleuzianism, which is why I'm writing this. This is how Deleuze can evoke the infinite, the eternal, because it is a line that continues *before* and *to come*. This is also his Stoicism.

What I wish to add to this is that the transcendent also comes to cycle within the transcendental at a particular duration on the line of time, and this to me is Kierkegaard. A line with circles.

16 May, Zhuhai

I haven't kept up on the post-humanist thing because it seems like yet another technobabble discourse. I have such a hard time extracting technology from capitalism these days that I'm not interested. But I am concerned about the very real and imminent emergence of artificial intelligence. There will be no AI revolution because it is and will be sneaky. At some point, we'll willingly climb into our own battery-pods and disappear from the world to submerge into a non-world we name "world."

This, it seems in my darkest of moments, is what humanity wants anyway. A slide into the safety of a reasonable consensus, a soft and quiet place of ignorance, purity, the womb. It would mark a predictable resolution to the Enlightenment project and our growing obsession with reason in its war against faith. Funny irony: the reasonable embrace of scientific/mechanistic transcendence while laughing at those who believe in spiritual/divine transcendence, perhaps because science is seen as correct, faith as dubious. If there's one thing we don't want it's the feeling that we've been duped.

What would it be like if we all tapped into the network and achieved such universal consciousness, a universal ethics, a perfect trans-humanism? Subjectivity, a real subjectivity, could only occur in a mobile transcendence, a physical break from the habitual real into the forgotten real. (I suppose this is what the late Heidegger was writing about.)

Maybe at some point long ago nature made this decision, to adopt a universal ethics of ecology and evolution, and all of nature's life and lives had to succumb to it. Maybe there was a time before, when nature was subjective.

18 May, Zhuhai

Conservatism: Ethics determines morality determines law.

Liberalism: Law determines morality determines ethics.

31 May, Zhuhai

I'm not anti-capitalism. It's a great for spurring innovation and new products. I'm against capitalism that seeps into the souls of human beings and becomes actualized as the blood of ethics and culture. I'm against capitalism in education, in health care, in foreign policy, in domestic politics. All of these structures, ostensibly of-the-people, are not *infected with* capitalism, like an itch on the surface of the skin; they bleed capitalism on the inside, coursing daily, hourly, continually through the heart. We're its little thrombocytes and corpuscles, not the otherness of categories but the ones who pump the categories, we the attributes of its substance that pumps it like an oil rig and keeps it strong. *lub-dub. lub-dub. lub-dub...*

Why are we not outraged when protesters are beaten, why do we accept that unions are being eradicated, why do we accept a capitalist to lead our civilization, why do we freely choose one capitalist over another in the ritual of voting, why do we admire the success of business that exploits people? And when we're compelled to take action, why are we told to call our representative capitalist on the phone to complain?

> "the astonishing thing is not that some people steal or that others occasionally go out on strike, but rather that those who are starving do not steal as a regular practice, and all those who are exploited are not continually out on strike... why do people still tolerate being humiliated and enslaved, to such a point, indeed, that they actually want humiliation and slavery not only for others but for themselves? ...the masses were not innocent dupes; at a certain point, under a certain set of conditions, they wanted fascism..."
>
> - Gilles Deleuze & Félix Guattari[11]

---

[11] *Anti-Œdipus* (1977, Penguin). Here, the authors are paraphrasing psychoanalyst Wilhelm Reich.

15 June, Chiang Mai

To have information is to have been informed. Imperatives, slogans, directives, orders. You are told to believe in information. Is it any wonder then, that in the age of information, we have become incapable of thinking? We gather information as if this is the important task. But information, in its sheets and lines, comes to us in layers that muffle the silence necessary to think. There is little openness in the accumulation of information.

8 July, Chiang Mai

Tantalus is the pre-existential condition of mankind, of being imprisoned in the Underworld and knowing that life is beyond one's grasp, being able to see one's imprisonment and the objects of one's desire. Sisyphus is the post-existential condition, of the one who lives above ground, surviving in absurdity rather than imprisonment, of being given a task, a purpose, and continuing that purpose, freely moving.

11 August, Chiang Mai

If this time of thought is to be named "post-truth" or "post-facts," the loudest remedy seems to be "neo-expert" and "neo-consensus." It's a desire for a return to the innocence of a Walter Lippmann scientism. In a Lippmann world, the public is left at the very bottom of the power structure. Their role is to shut up and vote, while the experts tell them what's what. Strangely, this has somehow become the "progressive" response.

During the Clinton-Bush-Obama years, Lippmannesque media-scientism was winning, experts were dictating the dominant agenda through their media. During the Obama years the *deplorables*, feeling left out and giving in to racist tendencies, began to react against consensus facts and truth.

And here we are. Power pitting one segment of the public against the other rather than organizing around shared needs of basic decency. We've allowed power to siphon us, the public, into two equal and separate containers, with each claiming *its own* truth. Chaos is a ladder for those with the instruments to raise it.

If we want to get past this fucked up time, it's not enough to pray for a return to the Lippmann divide, to vote for its return. It would need to address why it is that *deplorables* no longer feel that consensus truth speaks to them. Because there is something real to feeling that something is not right with it, even if they don't have the words to put it in liberal-correct terms. The way people feel cannot be discounted because you want them to be analytical. The simple identity, that they are stupid, is a nonstarter. The problem has far more to do with the pervasiveness of media technology, income inequality, inauthenticity in politics, and a tech/science-obsessed education system rather than a humanitarian one.

What people want is to feel they are valued, that they have something to contribute. It would be nice if we could foster this. It would sure help as well if all of us were a little more tolerant of the beliefs of others.

14 August, Chiang Mai

A copy of Cornel West's "A Genealogy of Modern Racism" essay has been sitting on my desk for about two months.[12] Last night, after reading about and seeing the violence in Charlottesville, I figured it was a good time to read it. By offering a "genealogy" of white supremacy, West is suggesting that white supremacy is historically and culturally embedded in how one sees and thinks, nurtured by biases of history, science and images that uphold the normal and seek out the ideal of superiority. European and American white supremacy then is not a personal opinion, not a proclivity, not even a worldview. It's a condition of power—not the top-down power of authority, but the pervasive power of history, language, institutions and habits. Racism is conscious; white supremacy is unconscious.

By this definition, white supremacy is a ground out of which social constructions and attitudes congeal. Hate, yes, but also privilege and guilt, all of which might be motivating factors in efforts to remove or maintain the conscious, *visual* monuments of supremacy movements that whites would either fight to forget or fight to uphold. *Charlottesville*, as a moment, was much bigger than a statue, and the counter-protesters are heroes, on par with or even exceeding those of soldiers in war. They fought with their bodies. But my point here is that a monument is a visual identification. The fight about Robert E. Lee's statue was either to make it disappear (substituting the image for the problem) or keep it (keeping an object of supremacy visual). Either way it conceives supremacy on visual and conscious terms.

One would do well I think—I'm talking media here, social and corporate—to be careful in what one calls events like Charlottesville, especially if one is demanding a universal language of

---

[12] In P. Essed & D. T. Goldberg (Eds.), *Race Critical Theories* (2002, Blackwell Publishing). West's essay was originally published in 1982.

condemnation. Rather than white supremacy, one should instead call it hatred, neo-Nazism, Trumpism. Or maybe demanding a universal name is not what's important, rather facing up to our names, our discursive history, which lives in every American. It is a self-serving discourse, fed by an educational process that continues to prop up the ocular, legal and scientific standards that keep the idea of white supremacy alive.

15 August, Chiang Mai

My conception of cinema has fidelity to my conception of life, of travel, and of living in "foreign" places: *These are not my worlds.* I'm visiting. Wherever I go after this visitation, this life, this world, continues unknown to me. Every film I live moves on without me.

17 August, Chiang Mai

Normal isn't simply what *is*; it doesn't *happen*. It's *made* by what we accept.

*****

The attempt to unify is a strong one, but as we see in public rallies as well as in social media, it leads people to give their thinking over to a side and reproduce the statements and images of that side. It's how we allow ourselves to become mediated.

18 August, Chiang Mai

Why is Charlottesville the rupture it seems to be? Why was it not Fergusson? Fergusson seemed the more palpable, immanent fight. Charlottesville, with a bit of time now and hindsight, feels nestled in the problem of whiteness more than the struggle of equality. Charlottesville was when white supremacy came in conflict with itself. Here, "white supremacy" is not nationalism, racism, hatred, etc.; it is historical and indoctrinated—that which is educated. Supremacy in this historical sense is not a quality or virtue but a dominant and pervasive psyche.

In raising the question, then—why is this an event?—it is asked within the white narrative that continues, the continuing whiteness of CNN, MSNBC, FOX, Reuters, et. al. This is an issue of black lives. But even as corporations re-populate their newsrooms with ethnically diverse practitioners, the condition of white power remains. The institution of news media trains its practitioners, indoctrinates the practice, and the white narrative remains *the narrative*.

Charlottesville the lived event is different from the lived event of Fergusson. It was far more mediated in advance of its unfolding. In the aftermath, as it became the mediated event, it became a narrative moment when whites had to confront their own distorted mirror, a fracturing of this previously intransigent idea of supremacy that has survived this long. It was a white conflict: hate against shame. Shame doesn't invalidate good intentions, but it's more complex than standing up for equality. It's a situation in which a black story becomes colonized by a white narrative. This is how the news media functions—producing a mediated narrative for white consumers.

This is not to discount the potential long-term potency of the lived *and* mediated event. A lived-mediated rupture has its own reality that resonates. The point rather is that white supremacy was doing okay when the stories were of an African American struggle. Colin Kaepernick, Travon Martin, Fergusson: the record of events of late is incalculable. These were black stories that didn't implicate average white shame. These were perceived as top-down abuses of power: white NFL owners, white judges, white police. Such stories are easier to consume from a safe and removed distance. With Charlottesville, white supremacy is not just a witness to the other, but forced to face itself. This makes "sides" difficult to ascertain.

This is why Trump was right in two areas, although for all the wrong reasons: 1) There are many sides to this. There was one substance (white supremacy) but an impossible range of psychological histories. 2) Tearing down statues is not the answer. One can be against removing statues and also be on the side of equality and progress. But this is incomprehensible to those who ally and side. To put this another way, does an alliance with A or B only mean that one can stop thinking about uncomfortable complexities at work? The media narrative is that Jefferson is different from Lee because Lee was a traitor. This is not the reason of course. The difference is that Lee fought on the side that whites are ashamed of. Removing monuments feels like an attempt by whites to bury their shame, knock it down, hide it away. In one dramatic and highly public motion it is a very white-American thing to do, both pragmatic and symbolic. Further, it appeals to the law (in a rhetorical sense) to decide when to remove them, giving it institutional legitimacy. If one were to stretch the thought far enough, it is whiteness trying to preserve its own legitimacy, the supremacy of *its* law, its order and heroic honor.

Perhaps this is overly cynical, and perhaps unfair to other, real motivations, particularly by non-whites. There is also the element of whiteness trying to atone, to make amends, to repair what the Civil

War aftermath couldn't. The origin of statues is a particularly overt and racist manifestation of white supremacy. For this reason, they shouldn't exist in the first place. But today's *events*—the mediated stories told—aren't really about what these symbols are; it's more about who whites think of themselves as today.

The argument could be made that the statues should remain in visible consciousness, not buried to the realm of the unconscious and the unseen. If we take things at the level of psyche, which is what this is about, we should remember what we've done. That is, perhaps America should not forget itself, not just its supremacy but its inferiority, its mistakes—the entirety of American culture.

But I need to remind myself again, this is easy for me to say, this being my privilege to say. When I see the face of Robert E. Lee, I see differently. What black Americans must confront—visually, confrontally—is something I don't have to face. I cannot understand, for I have not *seen as this*. But I can sympathize. And I'm still trying to figure out how to think all this, to decide when to say something, and when to step aside and be silent. I write when I recollect the lessons of philosophy—that what is repressed survives and repeats, that all is in relation, that appearances both reveal and hide, that truth is a function of power.

What I worry about, what I've been concerned with since Trump took office, is the response, the *reactivity*. I always feel it is more important to criticize the response than to meme out the daily stream of individual horrors. I worry about the left and the center, the misplaced measures, the making sport of it all, rendering an idea of the fetishized and pre-framed *other* devoid of backstory or person. This is how we destroy ourselves, by fighting against each other, by placing salvation exclusively in these white rules of democratic law. At some point love does indeed need to enter the frame, to help us rethink what we've thought, to question our technology that spreads hate, and our education system that encourages the techniques of opposition and containment.

FRAGMENTS 3: 2018

7 January, Zhuhai

Entry date: 7 January, 2038.

Maybe what's happened is we all made the choice, somewhen, back in a time forgotten, to abandon the magical world in favor of this rational one. The choice seemed very clear then. The world of magic was unpredictable, uncertain, its power could be wielded by masters, upsetting the balance and sense of equality. Reason, on the other hand, was available to all. Rather than tapping into nature, one could develop one's own powers without the use of magic. Reason could allow societies to organize and produce new methods of thinking and new technologies, to advance science and health to extend immanent life. Transcendent matters could be abandoned if one allowed reason to accept that life is temporary, that it ends in death. Nothing mystical required, no afterlife.

Generations after entering into this world the path closed, awareness of the decision became lost. Like an arrow, we were shot into the world of reason. But worlds don't die. This other world retained its character and resonated into the unconscious. As we accepted science and technology we began to feel, collectively but in various individual manifestations of denial or openness, an ineffable sense of loss, an anxiety without object.

Magic began to creep back into life even as we denied it. Through the fragmentations of digital experience in the proliferation of technology, reason became fragmented. At first these ruptures were dark and sinister, as cracks are when worlds re-emerge. Data began to lose its predictability, devices built for convenience began to strip us of presence to the moment, the availability of information ushered in not the promise of knowledge but the abuse of understandings. Politics consolidated opinion into hardened polarities, democracy failed as technology became a tool of power for the powerless, as a result of it being used as a tool of entertainment and communication for the powerless.

All along we could feel this, we could feel the resonance of lost magic, we could feel that something was off in the denial of spirit. Feelings were not welcome in a world of science, technology and reason. We didn't begin to see it until America somehow elected a product of technology and media entertainment as its leader. Even then it took decades to turn toward what was forgotten, as anxiety shifted toward action...

16 January, Zhuhai

My window into news events has become so narrow of late, mostly coming through the snipes, guffaws and links to profit-based media sites. We seem to be firmly in the age of identity now and I find myself fascinated by the questions and seeming contradictions it raises. One is told to respect the category, yet also to stop trying to make a statement on the category unless one belongs to the category. I have tried to write about these things recently but I am reminded by friends that I cannot possibly understand. They cite my whiteness and maleness as the cause, the root, of such incapacity. Men who try to contribute to a discussion of feminism may only show alliance, and must stay clear of the interjection, the chasm, of "mansplaining." If I suggest that perhaps my perspective may have as much to do with my *experience* as my identities, I am told that this is white privilege. This is where the conversation ends, this synonym for "shut up."

We are living in a time of political uncertainty unlike any other. There is real anxiety in the social media sphere of information, facts and events. What was once lived and exchanged has become digitally scattered. The speed of these lines makes it impossible to reflect upon what's occurring. So much of this production manifests as hatred, racism and misogyny. The response is to retreat into one's identity. It's become the digital version of an instinct, akin to survival. Such reactions are understandable when one feels the patterns of attack and oppression that are very real, and occurring on a daily basis. This is the pervasive condition of patriarchal dominance that leads one to gather and produce an opposing force. But there is also harm done when those who close on identity demand that others *must do the same*, leading to the harmful reaction. We hear of a "teachable moment," but it carries the weight of blame that inhibits learning. In minds susceptible to hate, this might spur a counter-retreat to racial animosity. This is how resentment and counter-resentment functions. It feeds on conditions of oppression that lead to reactiveness and opposition.

Philosophically, the difference here is one of *being* and *becoming*. Identities retreat into being. Being deploys facts to preserve itself. Another strategy is to consider an ethics of becoming, that it is possible to transcend (in the existential sense) one's condition. This is why continental philosophy often concentrates on "-ing" words like thinking, feeling, opening, rupturing, etc. The identity that fixes into stasis is the enemy to all of this. In part, this is because this effort toward being removes the philosophical questioning that must continue; but also, and related to this, the identity established becomes itself corruptible to the forces that continue to surround it.

That is to say, power as being is far more problematic historically than power as becoming. In a regime of identity as a mandate, philosophical discourse is marginalized. It's also why philosophy is more important than ever. It's able to *create* language and other lines of expression that deterritorialize identity in a way that science, law and religion cannot.

Becoming is a concept that resonates in feminist philosophy. But social media feminism seems to have forgotten the power of Simone de Beauvoir's famous quote: that one is not born but *becomes* woman. This isn't a self-help invitation, and the quote cannot be isolated from Beauvoir's existentialist effort, which is to describe, genealogically, how society conditions a girl to become "a woman" in patriarchal society. The process has no goal, it is the conditioning element which any *existential* woman struggles to transcend, that is, to *become*. This double meaning of becoming is no accident.

There is a different take on this from Gilles Deleuze who, with Félix Guattari, writes of a distinction between the *molar* and the *molecular*. Being and identity are molar; becoming is molecular. They do not entirely advocate for the molecular, because that would leave us scattered, in chaos, unable to reterritorialize. Instead, they are creating discursive concepts to describe two activities, which we can then extend to conscious thought and action. The molecular is where things move, gather speed, recombine. What I see in social media feminism (what's being called "fourth wave") is a molar activity by women and men to reproduce an identity of *woman*, to *find* woman. Molar strategies are about overcoming power with power, overcoming being by instituting another regime of being.

Becoming, on the other hand, is for Deleuze and Guattari always a "becoming-woman." All becoming is female and molecular: "the animal, flower, or stone one becomes are molecular collectivities, haecceities, not molar subjects, objects, or form that we know from the outside and recognize from experience, through science, or by habit."[13] The being of man is the dominance of male agendas, but there are no "becomings-man." The gender *identity*—the molar, the being—is not essential to the concept. Both women and men enact being-man when identity, subjectivity, science and habit are emphasized. This is because "man" is always the majority, the dominant (the patriarchy). Events enact male agendas when the molar attitude dominates, which is prevalent in communication, media, science, etc. But the way out is not to oppose; this merely sets up a binary, an opposition that maintains the dominant structure. A feminism of difference instead encourages seeking out *another* expression. To *be* anew is first to become. As D&G write: not a "natural" relationship (between A and B), not an opposition (A against B), but an act of "production (from A to *x*)."

This extends as well to the problem of white supremacy. D&G mention how the Black Panthers didn't advocate a being-man, they instead needed to *become-black*. For minority expressions to rise, they must *become* as a means of transforming the identity of being. White supremacy, as with patriarchal dominance, is the molar condition we all live in. Like the molar-male, white supremacy is what has been built; it is what we all live; it is The Law as historical. To overcome it, there must be expressions and discourses that deterritorialize it. Molecular expressions of becoming-black must be allowed to thrive; this can be said as well of becoming-woman.

Social media is dominated by identifying and opposing expressions of someone like Donald Trump. A molecular/becoming approach would be to instead create expressions that are themselves "minoritarian," regardless of the identity of the one who expresses. D&G write:

---

[13] Gilles Deleuze & Félix Guattari, *A Thousand Plateaus* (1987, University of Minnesota Press). All quotes and paraphrasing in this entry come from their Ch. 10.

"It is perhaps the special situation of women in relation to the man-standard that accounts for the fact that becomings, being minoritarian, always pass through a becoming-woman. It is important not to confuse 'minoritarian,' as a becoming or process, with a 'minority,' as an aggregate or a state. Jews, Gypsies, etc., may constitute minorities under certain conditions, but that in itself does not make them becomings. One reterritorializes, or allows oneself to be reterritorialized, on a minority as a state; but in a becoming, one is deterritorialized. Even blacks, as the Black Panthers said, must become-black. Even women must become-woman. Even Jews must become-Jewish (it certainly takes more than a state). But if this is the case, then becoming-Jewish necessarily affects the non-Jew as much as the Jew. Becoming-woman necessary affects men as much as women. In a way, the subject in a becoming is always 'man,' but only when he enters a becoming-minoritarian that rends him from his major identity."

This points to the problem with aims toward "correctness" as the new puritanical attempt by liberals to correct our language and our terms as a means of correcting the object, the being, of irrationality and hatred. In this, we engage in the absurd effort to correct the *representation* that stands for the thing, since we are unable to approach the object. From a pragmatic standpoint, such an oppositional dialectics will only polarize. From a value standpoint, it functions as a controlling method. Its intent, genuinely aimed toward equality, also pushes to establish a regime of permissible and impermissible expression. Thinking in divisions of being, the molar strategy, produces a molar result—who is inside and who is outside. In other words, it is an establishment of power against power.

This helps to understand the problem of Hillary Clinton and the support behind her. There is an element of "being-man" to her representation—majority, molar, dogma, status quo. Clinton is a woman who is also being-man in enfolding the practices of male dominance. This, unfortunately, is the incredibly difficult situation women of stature face, as Beauvoir chronicled. Does any woman's success in a man's world require being-man? Bernie Sanders did not have to face such a difficulty. He is a man, but he was also enacting strategies of becoming-woman, becoming-minority. He was the rupture, the new thinking, the process that stood against the molar identity that is the Democrat/Republican binary. It was not merely about him; his movement and the movements which resonate with him were all becoming-activities against the established territory. This is a threat to State control. So when the molar agent—the Democratic Party power machine—actively eliminated becoming-woman, many chose to remove themselves from the choice that remained.

This is the problem in which the progressive movement finds itself post-Trump. It has chosen molar modes of legislating identity and correctness through strategies of reactivity, opposition and regression. It functions in terms, names, semantics, laws, and a presumed order of higher reason. It is attempting to contain chaos rather than embracing the shifts and movements of becoming. In January, we promised resistance; this required that we *unsettle* things, not settle them. Resistance must be female, rootless, *rhizomatic*; it must become woman.

It's important to reiterate the advantage, indeed the privilege, that Sanders had over Clinton. As a man, he had the privilege of becoming-woman because he *is man*. She doesn't have this privilege and is subject to higher scrutiny in any becoming-expression. Additionally, it must be said that I am also man, with the privilege of attempting to write a becoming-woman relatively free of such scrutiny. I am in the molar position of privilege to advocate an expressiveness of becoming against the dominance of man. But perhaps as well, this gives me a *different* position from which to write, to make a plea for becoming-woman. It is not enough for men to ally; we must also express lines of feminism that harmonize the effort to upset drives that continue the oppositional molar dominance.

Woman is not any one thing, nor is feminism. Its many threads can open to multiple possibilities. We must continue to fight against the assault against individual women. But we cannot forget other possibilities, ones that move at different speeds, ones that unsettle and become, and which do not turn toward being-male in an effort to release us of its dogma, a dogma which *must* be unsettled.

2 March, Zhuhai

If I were to attempt to boil down the vast breadth of western philosophy into an overly simplistic equation, I'd say that at the personal or existential level it attempts to bring to light the incalculable variations in questions of programming versus instinct, culture versus animal; from this, the degrees of freedom one has to rationalize one's very sense of individual will; and finally, how language both informs and is drawn from the desire to express the power of one's will.

What I find happening today, in a world that has abandoned philosophical inquiry, is that individuals are actively discounting the incalculability factor. Because of this, there is little accounting for the fact that we are *both* programmed and instinctual, both culture *and* animal. The will to freedom or power then is calculated through a firm belief in whatever *is*, which is a matter of faith. Faith in God, faith in science, faith in reason. Because one is constantly told to believe in oneself (there's that programming again), one has already chosen before one is given a chance to think. One thinks one is thinking, but one is often merely legitimizing one's faith born of an incalculable whole of forgotten experience.

Philosophy is meant to break this apart, to re-gather such incalculables in the form of concepts for thinking. (I suppose therapy plays the same role; but even therapy seeks to find a cause when there is likely no single cause in a temporal web of forgotten events that all resonate each other.) Philosophy has given way to science, whose job is to calculate. At the level of society, ethics has given way to morals, as thought has given way to laws. So many rationalists out there, forgetting that the overwhelming majority of who one is has long been forgotten.

9 August, Dublin

I'm sitting in the Dublin airport waiting for a flight to Poznan and reflecting on some time spent with family in Virginia Beach. There's something that I adore about the American South that is difficult to pin down. There is that term that recurs, "Southern Gothic," but I'm not sure what that is either. The south feels old, it feels vaguely haunted. Everywhere there is a forest that beckons; if I stop to look into it, it seems to be staring back at me. Each acre not only has its story but its time-slices of stories: forgetting and loss, sadness and horror, joy and innocence. I'm romanticizing of course, but it's something I feel.

There is also my fascination with American history, particularly the Revolutionary and Civil wars. There past a rush of cars and SUVs moving down a busy boulevard is a slight rise in a field that might have been a scouting location for a small cavalry band. Everywhere to me is a possible battleground or path that moved armaments into position—reinforcing, retreating, relocating, reassessing. Death, strategy and landscape, these are the aspects of war that I find compelling.

Virginia was America's first colony. It's also where the majority of my family is now, since my father passed away. Virginia

Beach is a massively spread out metropolis of military and surf culture with no discernible downtown. An LA of the south, but without the creative industry and not a single sign of anyone freaky, artistic or leftist. It is mostly made of soldiers and families, a different America for me. I'm Californian to my core, but even that state feels foreign to me, an expatriate for more than a decade. California for me is a different landscape—all beauty and few ghosts, at least to my tendrils. It's a place of artists and free spirits, liberals and leftists, hiking and cafes. I know it well, I feel comfortable there. I can get around without a car; at least in the Bay Area, I can walk.

Virginia is not California. And this leads me to the less appreciative aspects of this reflection, but things I want to note because Virginia, as charming as it is and the place of my family, also embodies the world that is alien to me. This, in so many ways, is America, this Virginia, which inspired the following conclusions:

1. Ownership is everything. This falls into two areas but resonates everywhere: There is personal capital, the ownership of cars, houses, weapons, wealth, all meant to satisfy the needs of the present to combat the anxiety of possible future loss. A house is not only a place to live, a car a means of transportation; they are investments, accumulation, credit. Together they congeal into points systems in substance, and iconography in appearance, which together comprises "citizenship." There is also the collective capital, which circuits constantly back into the personal as referential, each upholding the other under the same rubrics. If someone questions capital in its "ism"—as corrupting the university, the arts, our very souls—such a person is heretical, because capitalism is the blood of both the collective and the individual body. To criticize the system is to criticize the universal aim of life.

I feel ownership when I'm in Virginia because I am happy to have little. I neither possess personal capital nor feed the collective capital because I am outside of the state and the nation. To feel it, to enter into it, after years living outside it, is particularly affective. In Virginia, walking down the street feels unsafe for a variety of reasons. First is because of the ownership of cars. It was particularly acute on this visit that drivers show little care to pedestrians like me. Walkers and cyclists are foreign creatures, ones which evidently live outside of ownership and do not buy into capital. Perhaps it was my imagination but drivers deploy their cars as if they were weapons, or rather bullets. I was discussing with a friend recently that while I'm in a Buddhist country, cars adjust to get out of someone's way. But in a nation and state that places rule of law above all else, these personal metal boxes with wheels move as if shot from a rifle. They move too fast in perfectly straight lines, in accordance with the laws. I don't care if that guy's crossing at a crosswalk, he's outside of capital.

2. "Public" is a transcendent concept. By transcendent I mean it exists in idea only, separated from the immanence of lived experience, and therefore holding little regard. Public begins and ends with measures of distance: voting, charity, philanthropy, taxes. These things are mostly done in private and are secured in the end with a signature. All are infected by money, transcendent money, money that moves through automation. How many public goods are left? Media: capitalist. Health care: capitalist. Transportation: …

Transportation is the one that hit me personally on this visit, not only because of the danger of being run over, but because it was impossible for me to use public transportation in Virginia. When I bought a flight from Dublin to Dulles, I assumed that there would be *some* public transportation to get me across the 200 miles that separate it from Virginia Beach: a train, a bus, something. This is where Asia and Europe have spoiled me. Public transportation is what the living public uses. But in America, since everyone *owns* a personal metal box with wheels, bus stations and train stations are left to the poor—those devoid of capital, living outside of ownership. There was simply no easy way to get there without renting (buying for a day, and bearing all legal responsibility for) a metal box with wheels.

3. <u>Racism is in the psyche</u>. Virginia Beach not only has no long-range routes for public mobility, they are also lacking in short-ranges options. There is a very limited bus system, but from what I was told I'd need some kind of monthly card. I learned that recently there was a measure up for vote in the city to create a light-rail system for the town. This would have brought the oceanfront neighborhoods in reach with the more affluent suburbs. But the measure failed. And herein lies the racism within democracy. Would middle-class suburbans have loved to reach the beach by light rail? Those with wheeled boxes, maybe less so, but for the young, sure. The problem was the other direction. Many areas of the oceanfront are populated by black people. The fear, and the reason (at least in part) that the measure was shut down, was that blacks would have easy access to their private property.

Black people are sometimes seen by whites as lacking capital, living outside of ownership. Perhaps there is some element of truth to the stereotype in individual instances, given that racism is systemic, operational, pervasive. And the response to this is apparent as well. Many black people I saw in Virginia, not all, look to my white eyes as imposing, even threatening. The discontent is real. So this is the cycle: whites carry privilege and (some) blacks respond with anger to this reality. The odd change recently is that whites don't even hide their racism anymore. Part of this is Trump, but I think people are just more aware of everything. The suburban racism is just how things are. Whether at the macro or interpersonal level, in violence or in awareness, racism lives even without anything said or acted. It moves through everything; it's in the psyche. This makes it easy to foster that other distance, the distance of *other*. Racism keeps the other as other, separated from what is privately owned.

4. <u>Things are far too large and relationships far too distant</u>. The above three observations—ownership, publicity and racism—resonated strongly in my regular walks through neighborhoods that weren't mine. I seemed to be an object of confusion. There was the

neighborly "hello" which comes partly as a genuine salutation but almost as well a defense mechanism against... against what? Accusations of being unneighborly? A possibility of violence? It felt at times that to face the stranger is a means of disclosing his intentions. (I often wondered in such a hello: who is paranoid, them or me?) I was a strange object indeed: my "other" was white (good), but with long hair and a beard (not bad but at least suspect in a military city). I cannot blame them. Were I in the situation of preserving my ownership, I would deliver the same "hello."

There are also lovely little lakes in these neighborhoods, with little parks at intervals around the perimeter—swing sets, sand lots and benches. But all of them, every single one, had a sign that read "Residents only: Trespassers will be prosecuted." This was unfathomable to me, that a lake and a park is private rather than public. And then I remembered: right, the black people. Lacking publicity, benches are free from the non-owners, the property-less, the home-less. I regularly violated this rule, knowing full well that even though I am bearded, metal-box-less and long of hair, whiteness gives me the privilege that dissolves the instant of actionable doubt.

Complementary to the emergence of digital technology and social media, the discursive universe is massively spread out. The otherness that one deals with is more distal than proximal. This is completely different to my life in Asia. In China, Thailand or Korea I deal only with what is local and interpersonal. This brings its own problems, but the other stands before me. In the States, nothing feels close because everyone is speaking, making it hard to listen. The proliferation of noise leads to a total silence, a mass inaction. This isn't just political, it affects neighborhoods, creates competition, builds suspicion. I will give this to Virginia: neighborhoods still exist. But they are contaminated by distal noise that comes close in anxiety: doors are locked, kids don't play in the street, privacy is holy.

I'm starting to come around to the idea that such problems may be mollified when we begin thinking at the level of smallness. Small is what is actionable, immediate. It collapses otherness into a neighborhood of *persons*. I notice that when people discuss things in person it usually goes well. What creates animosity is the conceived wholeness of other categories. America is such a category, and it's why I'm concentrating on one state, one city, one neighborhood. The reason people are suspicious is not because someone is walking down the street; it's that at the *national* level, fear is peddled as a commodity, as capital. One buys one's paranoia by streaming information produced by privately owned national news corporations. Its content feeds abstract fears through the images of others: blacks, Mexicans, refugees, liberals, conservatives. I wonder if instead, discourse should reduce to one's locality. Interactions should happen at the level of the state, the county, the city.

Despite the clamoring about late-stage capitalism, I don't see it ending without catastrophe. Maybe that's what the clamor is about. But if capitalism ends, all this rumination I'm doing is meaningless anyway. I believe however that the other three things I mentioned above are malleable. There's something to the psychology of dissolving otherness through interaction. It's a simple, very social-science, very humanist approach, but if we're to save ourselves—not our ownerships but our souls—I think community may be a path forward. It's something I'm working on for the future.

23 September, Zhuhai

Liberals are the new conservatives.

Alt-right are the new radicals.

This revolution sucks.

30 September, Chiang Mai

As much as I try to fight it, because it seems such a simplistic, convenient and contained worldview, I do subscribe to the aquarium theory of existence. This suggests that the limitations of reality (from consciousness to the cosmos) is somehow "observed" by a higher entity. We name it as God or various other spiritual traditions because we cannot understand it. All we can do is name.

I don't like that I like this because it seems to necessitate a transcendent existence, something residing outside of experience. I'm a firm believer in immanence, even in the case of infinity. But maybe it's not outside; perhaps we do access but we need to learn to listen in different ways. The reason I subscribe to it because the concept of scale makes sense to me. I have wider field of awareness compared to the ant (so we presume), so why not continue the scale?

If this is the case, then intelligence and knowledge are probably best conceived not as being contained in the mind but are names for a force. The Greeks pondered this: a floating *nous* (intelligence), a nonlinguistic and evolving *logos*, a Pythagorean *harmonia* with dissonance, the grand *apeiron*. Such a force or power of knowledge is then akin to gravity and it becomes a matter of degree and localization. Here, the grain of rice falls to the floor in a highly localized event whereas the Earth moving around the sun is occurring on a grander scale. And on upwards, but into realms beyond sensation and perception. Why not knowledge too? Circles and rotations seem to be a familiar pattern, as is repetition with differences in each manifestation. The mind cycles and repeats, as do the planets. What else cycles?

I don't pray to any entity beyond the immanence of nature. But I do give thanks in my own way. There are horrors, genocides and plagues, but these are grand-scale names for what is lived at the small, localized scale: trauma, suffering, sickness. I don't know why any of this has to be part of the process. But that's because *I don't know*. I'm a grain of rice grateful that I have a bed to sleep in every night and friends I can call on when things get shitty. The thanks I give is for the little nudges that keep the aquarium from imploding completely—the poke of this twig here, the movement of the seashell there. The lightbulb is still on, the electric bill is being paid. Whatever we can say about history and its disasters, the Earth remains a home —at least for now.

6 October, Zhuhai

"Yes we have to be united. But when we have at the same time this alt-right rebellion, whatever you call it, the crucial point is, what did we—insofar as we count ourselves liberal, progressive— what did we do wrong? ... Trump is doing his job of successfully ruining, gradually, the Republican Party. The Democratic Party, what are they doing? All these stories about Russians meddling, of course they probably did, the way the United States are doing all the time in foreign elections. But this was not the crucial factor. The crucial factor, it was clear, was the mistake—the totally wrong strategy, getting rid of Bernie Sanders on the left. All this obsession with Russian hackers and so on, it's just to prevent [us from] asking the key self-critical questions. The real way to fight alt-right and Trump is to go on with this self-critical side. If we don't do this and just believe, and just trust guys like Jon Stewart and John Oliver, then we can have all the laughs at Trump. But he will keep winning."

- Slavoj Zizek[14]

News articles will explain what's happening to the US, to "us." But it won't ever explore the conditions that have led us here. Social science can conduct its tests, apply its models. Evangelists who have taken sides thump about the transcendent demand for a vote, a patience for justice that carries about the same amount of weight as a prayer. But we might also want to step out of the language of explanations, models and prayers for a while, find time within all that webclicking, to read some books. Because the sad passions abound through our repetitions and cycles; they are not limited to any side.

"one should ask rather precisely *who* is 'evil' in the sense of the morality of *ressentiment*. The answer, in all strictness, is: *precisely* the 'good man' of the other morality, precisely the noble, powerful man, the ruler, but dyed in another color, interpreted in another fashion, seen in another way by the venomous eye of *ressentiment*."

- Friedrich Nietzsche[15]

"The tyrant needs sad spirits in order to succeed, just as sad spirits need a tyrant in order to be content and to multiply. In any case, what unites them is their hatred of life, their resentment against life."

- Gilles Deleuze[16]

---

[14] I transcribed this quote without taking note of the source. It's a public speaking engagement given sometime between the election and this date. I searched but could not find the link.

[15] "On the Genealogy of Morals," First Essay, s11, in *On the Genealogy of Morals and Ecce Homo* (1989, Vintage Books).

[16] *Spinoza: Practical Philosophy*, Ch. 2, sIII (1988, City Lights Books).

"We may both love and hate the same object, not only by virtue of these relations, but also by virtue of the complexity of the relations of which we are ourselves intrinsically composed. ... We seem to be determined to much contest, much hatred, and to the experience of only partial or indirect joys which do not sufficiently disrupt the chain of our sorrows and hatreds. Partial joys are 'titillations' which only increase our power of action at one point by reducing it everywhere else. Indirect joys are those we experience in seeing a hated object sad or destroyed; but such joys remain imprisoned in sadness. Hate is in fact a sadness, itself involving the sadness from which it derives; the joys of hatred mask this sadness and inhibit it, but can never eliminate it. We now seem farther than ever from coming into possession of our power of action: our capacity to be affected is exercised not only by passive affections, but, above all, by sad passions, involving an ever lower degree of the power of action. ... We come closer to our power of action insofar as we are affected by joy."

- Gilles Deleuze[17]

24 December, Virginia Beach

Puppy chasing its tail: canine version of the mirror stage.

---

[17] *Expressionism in Philosophy: Spinoza*, Ch. 15 (1990, Zone Books).

FRAGMENTS 4: 2019

4 March, Virginia Beach

Much of philosophy is a decision of what to refer or relate to, not in terms of authors or texts (although that's part of it too) but in terms of life. Science refers to its process as visibly empirical. Philosophy, so often, refers to what is outside and what is unseeable and unnamable. This is why, the more I read and write and think, the more I'm drawn to mysticism, itself a dwelling relation in thought (and in listening, neither seeing nor understanding) to what is open, outside, unnamable and real.

8 March, Virginia Beach

Interesting that translations of Nietzsche's metaphysical concept translates either as "eternal return" or "eternal recurrence." But in English, these are very different situations. Return has consciousness, there is usually some subjective element to what returns—to turn again, or to turn toward what again turns, in a similar or different way. Recurrence is event-based, life itself occurs again and repeats its cycle, emerging as the same or as a manifestation of difference. Return emphasizes the *self* in a situational position. Recurrence is the movement of *life* independent (although not separable from) any single consciousness.

I suppose it would be helpful if there were some term that overlaps the two into a braided experience. Life and consciousness repeating in some mutual transformation.

There is an element of rhythm to the term, given the eternal. There is not a single repetition but life *cycles eternally* in repetitions. The meter of this rhythm, its pattern and its soul, goes beyond human sensation and cognition. The rhythm is too slow for even the attentive mind. In the midst of a repetition, one is only aware of this instance, this moment. But one is also aware on some level that life and self are happening again. The soul knows what the mind cannot, and for action to find its grip in the repetition, the spirit of awareness must pull something forward, to change the beat ever so slightly, to advance the song, to mutate the chorus.

16 March, Virginia Beach

As I work through philosophy, in writings and readings I want/need to do, there are two recurring metaphysical themes:

One has to do with concepts of the *outside of thinking* and the possibilities therein. Philosophy has many names for this, usually as a response to Kant's Transcendental Idealism: "the unconscious" (Freud), the "virtual" (Bergson, Deleuze), the "outside" (Deleuze, Foucault, Blanchot), "language" in the sense of its totality.

The other is that of the unseen and unknowable life-force that drives and binds action. From here we get the "*noumena*/thing-in-itself" (Kant), "will" (Schopenhauer, Nietzsche), "*élan vital*" (Bergson), "forces/powers/transcendental-empiricism" (Deleuze).

Then there are the concepts that overlap the two. "Forms," "*logos*" and "will" (as subjective) for example. These conjoined concepts point to what is also often named as "spirit." This seems to center around Hegel even though I've read very little of him. Spirit is an interesting word in that in all these concepts, there is the question of what is immanent or transcendent, of what is available/accessible as a potentiality in this life versus what is (usually divinely) separated from life. The key word here is "life," a word of vitality that pertains to both thought and matter (as distinct from something like "the world" which is ambiguous, but usually connotes a materiality, one often divided from the self and thought).

Two interesting aspects arise from this. One is that these are often various naming schemes for what is ineffable and unseeable. Second, that concepts are vital to philosophy. "Concepts" here denotes not the correctness of naming reality, but of functional ideas working in a diligent, honest and careful manner. A concept so named is mutable, something to work through. For both of these reasons, philosophy is both valuable and frustrating. It is frustrating because the vitality lies in what cannot be answered (because it is ineffable). This runs counter to our contemporary demand for correctness and for answers. Philosophy is thus banished by today's intellectual set. What is valuable to philosophical inquiry is the continuing exercise of riding the question, which opens to new questions in the midst of uncertainty and the ineffable.

Most of what we live through cannot be explained; for philosophy, neglecting this leads to collective lapses at the level of ethics. We have to have the courage to think through what cannot be logically grounded. Certainty is the regime of today, from the most ardent scientist to the most devout zealot. Philosophy is not a practice of certainty. It is, ultimately, a practice of ethics.

23 March, Virginia Beach

We don't speak language (animals and insects speak language). We speak functions. We speak purposes. We use words to string together *affects*, to control, to pet.

29 March, Virginia Beach

Our sacks of biology are at war with information. We thrive instead on nourishment.

*****

Stoicism: acceptance of suffering

Epicureanism: liberation from suffering

No wonder Stoicism is the hip fad in business culture. Screw that. Be Epicurean. Limit your desires, enjoy time with friends, live the joy.

5 April, Virginia Beach

Our collective neurosis is a direct result of the social demand for reason.

*****

Thinking of Blanchot...

The reading that helps is the one that hurts.

7 April, Virginia Beach

Imagine that mathematics only studied and produced works on geometry. Imagine science only studied and produced works on chemistry. Imagine philosophy only studied and produced works on metaphysics. Our knowledge of these important fields would indeed produce knowledge, but would be woefully insufficient along the progress toward understanding life.

Now imagine there's an institution devoted to the public good, the documentation of history, citizen involvement, the possibilities and limits of democracy itself. Imagine as well this institution informed us about the world at large and our place in it, an institution that empowers citizens toward action, feeds minds with the parameters of discourse. This institution exists: the news media.

Imagine that this institution only studied and produced works on one person and the events concerning that person. It does this now. The news media *is* Donald Trump.

Institutions, sciences, fields, areas of thought and study, these are not transcendent entities, they are made by its makers. They are us. The institution of media is granted life by consumption, the *us* who consume it and through this, feed it. What we consume produces the product. In consuming Trump we are making Trump. In doing so, we feed and consume the institutions of advertising, though which we further feed and consume capitalism and wealth inequality.

This marks the conceptual point of distinction. There is Trump and there is Trumpism. Trumpism is not a person. It is an *ethos* that we have decided to live through our consumption and reproduction. In every joke, every meme, every shock and horror, every mention of presidential politics, every mention of defeating him, every other reproduction that we take joy in producing, we together contribute to its actualization, and thus its power. Our laughter and our ridicule, our impassioned outrage, empowers it. This is not the fault of Fox News, CNN, the New York times. They are doing what they do because it generates wealth and makes a few rich people very, very rich. It is not even the fault of Donald Trump the person, an opportunist "reading the room." Fault lies with the choice to consume he who is the media, "it" that is the discourse.

This is the problem of dialectical thinking, that of oppositional power to the dominant power. Left versus right, Democrat versus Republican, or even deeper, superior intellect versus inferior intellect. Every negation legitimizes the power of the dominant figure, the one who is master of the narrative and the institution. Our incapacities, frustrations, and sense of powerlessness to enact change comes from the dialectical fantasy that change may come from the contrast. Or perhaps we have no illusions of change; we simply want people to know that we, that I, am on the side of the good, the righteous, the enlightened.

To *resist* is to first admit one's own participation, to recognize how we, the "superiors," the "rational," made him and continue to make him. To resist requires *other* movements, other thought, other action, other expressions, other discourses. To produce such expressions of newness requires us to recognize the other that is not the opposite. Other conversations, other lines of flight, other thought, other art.

This consumption of media-Trumpist knowledge, because it is knowledge, it can't be all that we are. It requires creativity and discipline to move in other ways. It requires us, above all, to make the world we wish to be.

9 April, Virginia Beach

Taking a break from reading an essay about the life and work of Heidegger, I switch over to an essay found on Facebook lamenting the horrors of "post-truth" indifference...

Truth is not a thing, it's a question of one's sense of a relation to one's time and environment, of one's sense of living and having lived. Truth is social, concerned over what is immediately available, what one cares about and gives time to. What *is* is not truth. Rather, what we *do* is we gather thought (this active definition of *logos*).

This has always been my particular interest in philosophy, not a question of what is but a question of how thought gathers and how thinking is expressed. This is largely ignored today, with everyone chasing the object, a myth of the universal, the need to decide one's alliances *as truth*, a practical desire to give up and rest in the comfort of the truth one already possesses. There is no party or agenda in any of this, it's just the most convenient thing to do. To shift away from this, from attention on objects and one's truth to the continuance of thought, necessitates a dismantling within everyday experience, a different kind of preoccupation with thinking. *Dasein*. This clearing puts one "on the way" toward the possibility, never certain, of opening to a new truth (or in Heidegger's thinking, a very old truth reborn to thinking).

There's no such thing as "post-truth." There is no "indifference" to truth, rather indifference to the structures that claim it. Truth never was, its idea has always been made as a statement, a utility, a method of power, ideology and dogma. Perhaps people are smarter than we think, that somewhere in this capitalist-media jungle we "know" this on a felt level. Perhaps people are beginning to understand that truth belongs to its masters, that claiming it is a power grab, and that resisting it is an expression of freedom.

I'm thinking as well of an interview I watched recently with journalist Robert Caro, who said that we need to put to bed this concept of truth in the way people think about the word. His work does not deal with truth; his work is instead the rigorous discipline of dealing with facts. He too chases objects, which is what journalists do, but he is wise enough to admit that truth is out of the question.

As with truth, *facts* brings its own set of philosophical problems. But Caro at least recognizes the difference. There is one: both vast and narrow, chaotic and managed, that in the very effort to attain it, meaning becomes lost, or worse, dangerous. And there is the other: which journalists and scientists *can* work with. The problem here is the same: constructing arrangements of facts that pave an honest path toward something meaningful and actionable.

10 April, Virginia Beach

Waking from a dream...

My life is not the rock that juts out from the ocean, affected by the waves constantly crashing around me; my life is the ocean that crashes into rocks and moves life. This made perfect sense last night, not this morning. I think I have a higher opinion of myself while asleep.

Also, the ceiling fan in the bedroom I'm sleeping in now freaks me out. Sometimes when I open my eyes it's a clawed hand, other times a spider. Last night it was a court jester wearing a large flower hat, all limbs extended, frozen in time as it leaps above the bed to attack me.

11 April, Virginia Beach

"You cannot talk of colors to the blind. But a still greater ill than blindness is delusion. Delusion believes that it sees, and that it sees in the only possible manner, even while this its belief robs it of sight."

- Martin Heidegger[18]

19 April, Virginia Beach

There is no single or correct version of "feminism." There are instead many ways to think through it as a concept. Of the many possible paths, one distinction may be drawn: 1) a post-Enlightenment liberalism of European/American thinking, in which we take an individual as the fulcrum of any progressive action, as either cause or effect; this feminism is *reactive*. There is someone who objectifies the one who is objectified and subjected to; it is one of

---

[18] *What Is Called Thinking?* (1968, Harper Perennial). The German title better preserves the ambiguity of is-called/calls-to: *Was heißt Denken?*.

crimes, wrongs, laws and punishment; 2) an individual through whom an action itself progresses feminism. Here is an *active* relation of someone expressing something within a unique situation. It emphasizes an awareness of environments, locations, conditions, histories, other people. This latter aspect is the feminism commonly forgotten because it is not easily adjudicated. This feminism is about *expression*, giving rise to expressions, *this* expression. Both, among many others, are very real. But the former—in which the instance becomes a matter of collective justice and outcomes—gets the most mediated attention. What is this other feminism?

In my readings on Asian philosophy I came across this quote from Joel Kupperman:

"One of the features of Zen enlightenment, as we have seen, is heightened awareness of the detail and texture of the world. The average person will take in the broad outline of a fact: there is a woman or man doing such and such. Someone with successful Zen training, though, can pick up on a lot more than this, including psychological and spiritual qualities of someone encountered."[19]

There is a feminism in this, not because he mentions a woman, but that the former feminism mentioned identifies a woman as the fact of a situation, regardless of the conditions or the expression produced. Some popular feminist thought only sees "a woman" plus a "broad outline of a fact," as beginning and end, and establishes this as the ground of how feminism should be discussed. What Zen seems to suggest, and Taoism as well, is that we should also give attention to the expression made, which necessitates for a moment that one set aside the factual matter of gender and the instance. It's a different question: Does this expression—independent

---

[19] *Classic Asian Philosophy: A Guide to the Essential Texts* (2001, Oxford).

of but also inseparable from gender as identified—produce an active rather than reactive feminist power?

This gives rise to another question, does the writer have to be a woman for the expression to be feminist? The danger of a man taking a factual stance regarding women is one of authority. A very prominent male tendency is to render truth, fact, identity, correctness and authority into writing. There is a long history of this by writers who are men. But I also see, now, this tendency from writers who are women. Does the authoritative stance render a continued dominance of the patriarchal spirit through women? The feminism that interests me as a writer is the expressive one, no doubt in part because I do not suffer the violence of factual events. But I'm trying as well to get outside such facts, to the idea of expressions of feminine thinking, rather than to the identities of facts as a means of establishing power. I cannot know what it means to be a woman; I cannot reduce or explain her. Nor can I know what it means to be a person born in Korea or Japan. The question from this becomes: is a sympathy or harmony possible, in a musical sense? Can my lines be sympathetic to, and express in writing, a feminist or Asian thinking that I find to be valuable expressions of art and ethics.

The accusation here would not be of appropriation, a popular word in cultural theory now, but of essentializing. To assign essence to "the feminine" or "the Asian," is to exoticize, to divide. Philosophy, a feminist expression of philosophy, would instead do this work of synthesis and harmony, one that neither divides or effaces differences, but acknowledges and incorporates them. That is to say, I'm concerned that through digitally mediated forms, we are neglecting the power of an expressive feminism and are instead primarily interested in adjudicating issues of power.

22 April, Virginia Beach

I listen to ambient music when I sleep, when I write and when I read. It's there when I'm dreaming and when I'm thinking deeply. It tunes my mind to the meditative, even the spiritual, fibers and arrows of unconsciousness that keep me both focused and aloft. It narrows my mind to the thought that requires no language.

So I'm very picky about my ambient: no glitch, no "noise," no sudden sounds, no talking, no digital obstructions, nothing that scratches my spirit with cleverness. It has to stay still but also move, go somewhere, like a wordless conversation. It has to feel organic, be mostly arhythmic, and milk the rice-crispy synapses riding at the very top of my skull. I prefer duos and trios over solo artists (maybe a resonance of my teenage love for Tangerine Dream), and I like when there's guitar or some similar instrumentation to create these fibers of listening above or below all the hearing.

24 April, Virginia Beach

Karma is moral *anamnesis* in reverse.

27 April, Virginia Beach

Is the transition of *logos* from listening to reason an attempt to masculate the universe? Listening to the *logos*, listening to the woman-oracle as receptive process gives way to post-Christian appropriation: Word as authoritative, reason as active. It turns the feminine-empathy-mysticism powers male. The birth of man (the knower/seer who takes) from the womb (the woman/listener who gives).

17 May, Virginia Beach

Winter has come and gone. The game is over. As Daenerys Targaryen becomes the Mad Queen, I think of lack and desire, the mother and father in the child, the child who cannot create a child. I think of love and fear, the possibilities for a woman to transcend, and how being *in* belief, even love, can effortlessly, unconsciously weave one into the fabric of fascism.

Beauvoir writes of the possibilities of a woman's transcendence, of the capacity to go beyond one's condition. Men are encouraged toward transcendence all of their lives. This is their (our) privilege. For a women, it is much easier to conform to her given role of supporting her man and maintaining the possibilities of *his* transcendence. Beauvoir lays out the various arguments for why this is. The "eternal feminine" is not a conscious agenda constructed by men, it is a social reality reinforced by how women and men adopt the roles and repeat the cycles that maintain her subservience. Beauvoir is very different from so many of today's web columnists, who adjudicate and cast sentences. She instead is doing the rigorous work of Nietzschean "genealogy"—the unveiling of *another* history. From this work, she underscores the fact that women themselves are contributors in the continuation of this condition.

As *Game of Thrones* has concluded its disappointing final season over the past few weeks, I've also been working through Lionel Bailly's *Lacan*.[20] Jacques Lacan is someone I have encountered repeatedly in my readings, but I have read very little of his own words (it's the same with Derrida and Hegel for me).[21] Through Bailly's rendering of his structural concepts, it seems Lacan grants women more agency than Beauvoir. The latter places the problem at society and the need to change the systematic methods of programming to change the preconceptions that women bear. Lacan places things at the level of the psyche and the choices women have, opened through psychoanalysis. (To be fair, Beauvoir discusses psychoanalysis as well.) These are not mutually exclusive conclusions, but it's interesting that in Lacan "The Woman" does not exist as a universal, rather *there are women*. As Bailly puts it, for Lacan, "Boys seek to identify themselves in what they do, while girls tend to identify themselves by what they are." Men have little choice in the matter; but women do. All of this goes back to "the phallus" and the castration that young boys and girls face as they enter into relations with others—the laws and language of the symbolic realm.

Freud's Oedipus complex is biological; castration is about the idea of the penis, literally. "For Lacan, castration is the symbolic loss of an imaginary object—the phallus—which is the object of the mother's desire." The phallus is not biological but a metaphorical Other to be attained. This metaphor applies to both boys and girls; castration is "an acceptance that they haven't got the phallus." The baby's first relation is with the mother. S/he is powerless to oppose the mother, to impose her/his own will against the mother. There are different tendencies in the paths boys and girls take. The boy

---

[20] 2009, Bolinda Beginner Guides (audiobook narrated by Deidre Rubenstein). All quotes mentioned here come from this source.

[21] I've read Bruce Fink's *The Lacanian Subject* (1995, Princeton University), essays by Derek Hook and Dylan Evans, and I've studied him through courses at EGS. But I have not read any of the texts of Lacan's own words.

renounces the idea of being the phallus for the mother and identifies with the father. From this, he expects to one day bear the object that satisfies a loved one.

While the boy seeks phallic fragments, the girl has *options*. She recognizes that she is the same kind as the mother, so she can continue to identify with the mother. She will "inherit the mother's mantle, including the mother's desire for the phallus, which will be brought to her by someone else." The girl then doesn't need to possess the phallus in order to please someone else. She may instead choose to become the object of desire of the father, putting her in rivalry with the mother. She doesn't want to possess the phallus or its fragments, "but to attract someone who appears to have it."

In early infancy, both sexes identify with the mother. At castration, the boy realizes he hasn't got the phallus but also understands that he can no longer identify with the mother. He must find a new identity. The girl remains identified with the mother, so she remains in "Otherly enjoyment." This is terrifying for the boy; he is shut out. The girl is comforted in remaining in the mother-phallus relationship. She adopts the mother's "strategies in pursing satisfaction, knowing that one day she will be the mother." (We can again recall Beauvoir: how women *perform* their assigned sexual/ matrimonial roles, as is commonly done in *Game of Thrones*.) The boy dealing with castration, must seek for himself "by engaging with the Other." He can then identify with the father. The girl can also identify with the father, but has a choice in the position she takes. There is only one truly successful approach to dealing with castration for the boy. The girl can become the mother, but the boy cannot. Another way of thinking this is that boys go off on adventures in search of the phallus, while girls stay put, discerning who is the worthy bearer of the phallus.

In Lacan, masculine and feminine tendencies are not determined by biological sex. All men are subject to the phallic function (castration and all that comes from it). It becomes the object sought after. Because of castration, they form groups of Otherness, something else: football teams, organizations, finding meaningful groups, etc. Not all women are subject to the phallic function. Girls do not have to seek the phallus; they have the option of adopting the mother's desire as their own. The boy must find other ways of establishing identity, outside of the mother-relationship. He must become a phallus bearer like his father.

> "And as the phallus is an imaginary object, he must seek it in all his object-relations. This accounts for the great variety and randomness in so much masculine activity and inventiveness. Boys must find a place and a meaning for themselves, following the lure of the phallus and almost every square inch of the field of human life may be explored in this pursuit."

In girls, these are only tendencies. It's impossible to generalize about women because of the vast combination of possibilities with her castration. She may take on the phallic function or continue her mother's desire, constantly mixing one or the other or moving between one and the other. There is no single solution to the woman's castration. "This is why Lacan insisted that there is no such thing as 'The Woman'." There are only individual women, all constituted differently by the way each responds to castration. Lacan contends that a universal Man does exist because his path is set by his biology.

What does all of this have to do with *Game of Thrones*? Dany had a choice and she made it; or she had no choice and she did it for destiny. Her life and her choices are impossible for anyone to grasp; castration is tough.

One could traverse an existential or psychoanalytical analysis of any of the major characters of the show. But I write about Dany because to me, her path was the show. This is why, even with all the problems of the show's final season, "Dany's turn" has stuck with me and redeemed everything that came before and after. Dany's turn was Ned getting his head chopped off all over again. In that moment, I said silently to myself "ah!... shit, well... well yeah, of course." The criticism that it was out of character for Dany is misplaced. It was totally in character. In the moment of her violent turn, everything we knew about her but hid from ourselves emerged like a breakthrough therapy session. The anger over her turn was anger in ourselves at having believed in her, even though we knew all along who she was. (And we should admit, boys and girls, that much of the reason we believed in her was because of her beauty.)

Dany's turn was beautiful and tragic. I wasn't outraged at all but felt heartbreak for her. And at the level of narrative development, which I assume is Martin's, it showed that Tragedy is still alive. Tragedy is something of a lost art today, due to the overwhelming critical-theory analysis of how an identity is being *represented*. Caution over social representation destroys art. Today, women are only allowed to be written as victims or badasses, or are written in a way that erases gender from the equation (*ala* Rey in those horribly written Star Wars films). To use a scriptwriting term, women are rendered as "flat" characters. Dany was "round" because she was not a representation for anything. Her identity wasn't written, it developed and changed. She was always and consistently *becoming*. Dany was a complication of shifting identities within herself, moving along different desires—to be loved or to own the world, to wait for the phallus or to take it. She listened, demanded, gave in, asserted, trusted and distrusted. She felt her way through, following her belief in herself while shouldering the very real struggles of being a woman in a man's world, trying not only to transcend but to reclaim her destiny for all to admire. That she failed, that she turned, gives no satisfaction, and reminds us what it costs to carry any overwhelming burden. That *we* were fooled adds to the weight. Every fan had to come to terms with her turn—denial for many (blame the writer), or this realization that the truth about Dany's brutality was both there all along and *necessary* to get her this far.

There is something massive in this, a resonant political statement about the world in which we live: We were Tyrion and Jon; we were there *with her* for every step of the way, choosing to see hope while ignoring the imminent danger. It is a reflection for those who live with abusive partners, or who live as devout Christians or atheists, for those who pass their days intimately attached to a toxic friendship or an incremental fascist movement, even for those who believe that their superior and rational plans for the benefit of all can be realized. We lose the capacity to distance ourselves from what is so very close. This is how belief works on the psyche. It becomes unwittingly interlaced within the mechanics and expressions of power. By this definition, power isn't given to or born in someone but grows and moves through people, wraps itself around one's psyche and those nearby. This power moved through Cersi, through Dany, not because they were weak, far from it, but because their drive to transcend was coupled with desire to be loved, which, if we listen to Beauvoir, is a situation in which so many women find themselves.

5 June, Chiang Mai

So much of the philosophy of Nietzsche, Deleuze, Foucault and Lacan is to show that whatever is going on, there is always something else going on *at the same time*. This is not a dialectic; it is rather that any line, sequence, chain or process has an *and* to it that is neglected—the forgotten other that also lives, unseen or unheard. The ethics of their philosophy is to unearth these expressions that are very real but left out. Philosophy in this regard is an exercise in reclamation toward interpretation. History is not going to document it, science is not going to account for it, politics is not going to grant power to it. It's the work of philosophy to empower what is suppressed. And more, this suppression is not top-down but works at the individual level, the supposedly rational, conscious, pragmatic, utilitarian, moral, post-Enlightenment subject.

Doing the right thing, developing the right strategy, the proper statement, the correct solution, always leaves out those expressions that become forgotten. (In a sense, the right course of action is a kind of madness.) Like residue and resonance, these expressions are real, they remain. But as forgotten, they threaten to take on a kind of vengeance, not because they are "bad" but because they have not gained the power to be heard. But if given care, there is a joy in giving voice to what is forgotten.

18 June, Chiang Mai

I'm noticing a trend in recent philosophical/theoretical writings to emphasize that life is shared with others. Yes, true, we live with others. But we've forgotten what the poets told us: we mostly live alone, together. Most thinking cannot be shared, cannot be spoken. We can only speak language. But even here, although we know the same words, we often do not speak the same language.

I suspect this tendency has more to do with fearing a loss of empathy in our relations with others, which is a legitimate fear. But we would go a long way in realizing that the situation we find ourselves in today is about the thinking-that-cannot-be-shared, not what *is* shared. Why? Because the more we "share" in appearances and messages, the more we share at the level of approval, and the less we share at the levels of personal depth. We are broadcasters at the interpersonal level. Like the broadcaster, we hide truth for the sake of advertising a version of the self. Arendt was right: the ethical problems of living with others are problems of isolation and ineffability. Nobody speaks the same language. We all misunderstand.

22 June, Chiang Mai

The questions remain: the powers of self-awareness or the letting go of self-awareness? practicing inwardness or going outside? to live in the frame of modern discourse, idle talk, and sites of possible change, or to scatter one's consciousness into pure thought, pure chaos, into the vastness of the infinite whole?

It is either Schopenhauer's intuition, in which "everything is clear, stable and certain. There is no questioning, no doubting, no error: one does not want to go further, one cannot go further; in intuition one finds peace and in the present, satisfaction".[22] Or it is Han's reading of Nietzsche, in which "The just person listens to the things rather than to him- or herself. To refrain from having convictions means at the same time to refrain from oneself."[23]

The tension gives rise to an irreconcilable decision of what to do and how to be. To agitate or to resonate. Here we have a problem more suited to Zen than to the ancients of Europe: how to transcend while remaining in life's immanence. I'm hoping that somewhere in all of this is an "and" rather than "or."

---

[22] Arthur Schopenhauer, *The World As Will and Representation* (2010, Cambridge University Press).

[23] Byung-Chul Han, *What is Power?* (2019, Polity Press).

24 June, Chiang Mai

The modern US Democratic Party's political ideology is one of rationalism: the seeking of origins and causes and the supremacy of such thought toward resolutions. Democrat voters can't abide relativism, which is why they fear what they believe to be an "agenda" of postmodernism, and why they embrace writings of popular science and the correctness of statements. The relation of parts must be set aside in favor of a return to the whole. This is why Democrats are fundamentally religious thinkers, seeking essence in a world without God.

27 June, Chiang Mai

To a dog's mind, barking means getting paid. Some take their jobs very seriously.

*****

It's been such a pleasure to revisit Hume this summer in Chiang Mai. He's so clear in expressing his conceptions of how the mind works through memory, imagination, language and sensation in coming around to idea, belief, custom and habit. It's a reminder how much consciousness really just wants to close down thought to a decision and move on. The scariest thing to common thinking is the suspension of openness because of the danger of confusion. It's far more practical and safer to claim understanding than to risk not knowing. We work really hard to convince ourselves that we know, and in the process, we lose the capacity to learn.

This is more *thought from reading Hume* than Hume himself, but it's clear to me how important it is that we have positive experiences of events, because these impressions are what we habitually recall as ideas.

We tend to fix meanings to words. But conjuring an association from a word is an individual process, an act that moves along the experiences that gave us the impressions we associate with that word. Any word then means something very different to people who have lived different experiences. Everything is individuated.

It's odd then how we attempt to impose a generality on the thoughts of others. This to me is why we really need to tell good stories and not just go fact-hunting and inventing new logisms. Facts don't have impressions, so we can't expect anyone to *care*. This is, I think, in part why Hume de-emphasizes reason and emphasizes experience. Reason creates *its own cause*, from which truth is an *effect*. Reason creates maxims and laws, but it can only cycle back to customs already in play through reason. There is no imagination to pure reason.

A story, by contrast, is a fiction that engages the imagination in a creative interplay with memory. A story situates language and ideas in characters/people, an experience to care about and carry forward, one that leaves a good and lasting... *impression*.

28 July, Chiang Mai

To understand how we consume media, we should reflect on the lingering effect of how we made and consumed theater. In ancient times, theater/poetry used myth, passion, metaphor and allegory to *affect* an audience as entertainment but also as moral instruction and ethical complication. We see some of this played out very well today in cinema, literature, on stage, and in other forms, but those are seen as products of culture. Such narrative forms are contained by a receptive attentiveness. As contained, they are more of a private unfolding to personal experience.

News media has adopted many of the codes of narrative arts but transformed them into a chaos of information, facts, entertainment and public good. News is the *public* theater of today. But we lie to ourselves (thanks to the lie of corporate media) in believing that it is not entertainment and instead *necessary* for democratic participation. Watching images and listening to speech is deemed *participating*, with voting as the sole objective from the process of watching and listening. The *polis* used to gather in the *agora*, and later in the public sphere of cafes, to discuss and argue. While the stories of ancient theater/poetry provided an allusive ethical play of narrative and emotion, democracy as an act was separate.

Today, we have fused theater and democracy. We watch each other on tiny stages. There is no narrative, no story, just an endless series of topics. An actor stands on stage and an audience member shouts at him; another leaps onstage from the crowd and pushes the poet offstage, shouting counter-claims. There is no underlying *ethos*, no *mythos*, no character to connect with or pity. All that remains is passion. With no narrative thread, passion becomes unruly. This entertainment of news is the ground upon which we discuss and vote.

In a global society of data, information and facts, theater becomes not an allegory, but a *pathos* of data, information and facts. This theater is taken as real, and we grieve and become enraged over information. We have no time for oblique thought in this theater of information. In looking and speaking, we have lost the art of listening. What sad, soulless creatures we are.

9 July, Chiang Mai

The building of images in waking life is necessary for survival. So is the destruction of them in dreams.

18 July, Chiang Mai

Exhausted from yet another tired display of social media hatred against hatred...

You've all bought tickets to the show. You're all commenting on his show. You and he and us and them, in harmony, singing the endless commentary on his appearances and statements. Democratic presidential debates become about his appearances and his statements, the news cycle is his appearances and statements. We consume and regurgitate him to our entertainment and his benefit. This is *jouissance*, the excess enjoyment that becomes pain and suffering, but one that also empowers the idea to continue. Though *jouissance*, Trump becomes nurtured into *Trumpism*.

Stealing from Zizek: Trump is the last thing people see before they see class struggle. By constantly repurposing him and his image, we ignore real issues of class, income inequality and climate change, the three issues that are politically actionable and immanently threatening. So enjoy your *jouissance*, but admit that you're a content producer in doing so.

Trump's a racist? Shocking. It also has no relevance to core issues that are bringing on apocalyptic-level problems. What do I add by saying "Trump's a racist and isn't that just awful"? Nothing except to get applause from my own theater. In this X as a reaction to Y, there is an opposition of morals that masks a sameness in attitude, means and method. The game is the same—a continuance of sameness—and it's a game I do not wish to contribute to. This is why revolutions fail. If the *conditions* don't change, X vs Y only repeats the same cycles.

It's not that we shouldn't discuss race, it's that we shouldn't reproduce *jouissance* of Trump's racism, *jouissance* in the sense that it has no value. Meme'ing him is not action nor is it actionable. Economics and climate, these are actionable things. Meme reproduction is not active, not activism, not resistance. It is a participatory theater of *jouissance*. Trump meme reproduction, the enjoyment of his hate, is the theater of Trumpism. Let's all sit and stare and share and laugh and cry at the evil man on the stage we constructed together.

The uncomfortable (and un-*like*-able) reality is that anyone engaging in this game is comfortable. I'm comfortable. We sit here and have the privilege of debating these things on a computer or a smartphone. We liberals have expertly incorporated the correct language of our approved discourse that unites us as rational people. We oppose ourselves to the others, Them. Those people don't share or take part in this discourse, this language. We share the same flat world of technology. But they are barbarians against the higher *logos*. Together, we have fostered a reactionary atmosphere between those who speak the morally superior language and those who don't speak this language. In a discourse of otherness, there is no encouragement, only the pleasure and pain of judging. Liberalism has to own up to this and realize that Trumpism is the revolution of the outsider. Is Racism at the essence of Them? It's a dangerous presumption to make, but one often stated by the supreme rationalist. It is more likely that racial hate rises as a symptom of this division, of feeling displaced and blamed as "other," as "them."

By placing Them into a theater without putting Us there is religious thinking: good versus evil. Through social media, the Good *logos* presides over the Evil barbaric racist horde. But the garden is the same. Playing sport against the other does nothing but enrage all. The *jouissance* of rage. This is what sells media, the end of this game is the proliferation of hate and the generation of profit to the wealthy.

No one wants to talk about this, how liberalism fertilizes division and how the shared interests among people are sacrificed for the wealth of the wealthy. Class is entirely left out of the conversation. The Democrats used to be the ones who fought for us and them. The party has absconded. All it does now is react to Trump. And we're all complicit in this. It's his world and his game.

I'm not gonna play. It's the only resistance there is left.

2 August, Chiang Mai

It seems to me that the whole point of the *Phaedo* is to make Socrates feel better about dying. Immortality of the soul? The philosopher's soul is the best soul? Sure Socrates, sure, you're so clearly right, it's unquestionable. Drink your hemlock now. Fly like an eagle back to Hades. We'll take care of your *logos* while you're gone.

Either that or it's all one long allusion to penis size.

4 August, Chiang Mai

It seems a month can't go by without a new pop philosophy essay on the analytic/continental divide. I'm firmly, unabashedly continental. I prefer its *poiesis*, its creativity of thought in the development of ideas. In my admittedly limited experience, analytic writers tend to rigidly value correctness; continental writers tend to poetically re-situate all claims to correctness.

That said, a lot has changed since the 1960s and '70s. A lot has changed in just the past few years. These days, social justice and cultural politics writers too often don the fashion of continental/postmodern tendencies while aiming for an analytic fantasy. The way I'm seeing it played out, openness and critical thinking are not the aim. The aim is to institute a new normal regime of language that is critical as a means of argumentation. This is the influence of "critical theory" on popular discourse. Philosophical ideas become phantom terms to practice critique and analysis. Just as analytic philosophy aims to clear away the metaphysical bullshit in our rhetoric to get to clarity and reason, the progressive effort seems very concerned about establishing correctness to institute a new dogma. This critical thinking is less about critiquing the mechanisms of power and more about the establishment of power against power to enforce rules of a new society.

Equality is without question an important cultural and social issue, but it's not philosophy. Philosophy in its continental lines would never make a social demand. It would instead question power itself and how it is instituted. But with theory washing away its poetics, philosophical work becomes a series of namable assertions. This is why so many essays I read today assume a "truth" or "fact" and then move from this to judge anyone who doesn't adopt this same truth. It aims to establish the truth of names and terms, as with the analytic philosophers.

Perhaps this is why so many now want to dissolve the differences between what has been named as continental and analytic. This is a mistake. French philosophy was built on openness and interpretation, an ethics of shattering dogmas, identities, correctness, and assemblages that quietly assert domination over ideas, thought, art and bodies. Poetry and art (aesthetics) are vital to this process in the creativity of concepts and the creative play of language that makes allusions to draw out different thought processes. Americans reading French theory now, and arguing for a new rationalism, a new correctness, a with-us-or-against-us mentality, is utterly foreign to me.

Maybe it's the philosophers I read—Hume, Kierkegaard, Nietzsche, James, Bergson, Heidegger, Bachelard, Deleuze—who engage in the poetics of uncertainty, the fragmentations of belief, the creativity of ethics. Current political thinking has zero tolerance for this, for seeing things in terms of conditions, forces, powers, climates and other various states of becoming and agency. In the era of Trumpism, it feels as though everyone, including "philosophers," want to decide and negate, everywhere, on every "issue." The pace of such judgments is exploding. Events move so fast, there's no time to linger. Don't think. Act. Do. And then do the next thing. Now. Without openness, without lingering, thought—even the thought that thinks it is thinking—is dying, if not already dead.

Or maybe the true "continentals" are still out there, silent; maybe the French are holding on in silence while the Americans can't shut up about correctness. It's hard to tell when I'm awash in it, when it pummels me to conform. I miss the times I spent on the mountain in Saas-Fee, when thought felt free. It feels like ages ago.

7 August, Chiang Mai

As I read more about ecology lately, I've been going through some online articles on mindfulness. While I believe the practice has value, it carries the same problem as the current popularity of Stoicism, which places the responsibility on the individual rather than on structures of power. Mindfulness and today's appropriation of Stoic philosophy are perfectly paired with neoliberal capitalism and the digital nomad entrepreneur because they train the individual to willfully endure rather than face the more complex realities of social and socioeconomic conditioning. The stress in your life is not because you cannot deal, but because you are forced to compete. That is capitalism.

12 August, Chiang Mai

While reading Bergson's Creative Evolution, *a thought arrives...*

Science: all is given.

Religion: all is forgiven.

Or perhaps...

Science: all is given-for.

Religion: all is for-given.

*****

Knowledge and ignorance run the same course. They both see and are blind at the same time.

20 August, Chiang Mai

We live in a time of total knowledge, the zenith of the Aristotelian ideal. But it is Aristotelian in theory only, not in practice. This knowledge bypasses the senses to move straight into the mind. The change emerged slowly, as code replaced matter at the everyday functional level. The distribution of code along decentralized channels enabled the popularization of the Internet, which paved the way for the explosion of information and data gathering. Today we live a knowledge and information intelligence, which has usurped the sensory, the organic, the spiritual, and the material. Information is our discourse, knowledge is what we make, facts are what we consciously think.

We cannot access all of reality because we are humans narrowed by experience, memory and forgetting. We cannot access all of knowledge because power is still concentrated in the powerful. But we can access all of the information. That is to say, we know all that there is to inform us into an *idea of* knowing.

Knowledge isn't our problem today, not at least in the sense of a lack. The problem is that we remain organic creatures at the instinctual level, living in sensation, living as psyches. As this lived existence is underway, we believe we are not any of these things and we strive to discard them. Through it all, there remains a *pathos*, *ethos* and *arche* to life. These are our immanent ways of being, the ways we feel. Information and knowledge is the new transcendental frontier, fueled by its desire for more, which pervades everything at every level in a direction toward the future. God was both our divinity and our unconscious, as we read books and worked the earth. Knowledge/information is now our divinity and our unconscious, as we build data to earn money and gather facts to battle the ignorance of the imagined Other.

When it comes to social injustices, it's not surprising that the tendency is toward data and knowledge construction. We *comment* our acquired knowledge. We do so in data streams to replace communication, and gather and proliferate information to ascertain a truth. The heart is there, the belief in good intentions, but the sensation is lost.

I am closely watching and reading about the struggle for democracy in Hong Kong. What strikes me is their creativity and infectious sense of *will*. The Hong Konger has will because the individual *must* do this. There is an imminent threat with a deadline. They are creative rather than reactive, responding with their *organic bodies*. Americans, by contrast, lack creativity and will because they seem content to fight with keyboards. The spirit of struggle in the living sphere of danger and necessity are replaced by facts and the logic of argumentation. One active, the other reactive.

Perhaps it is because I'm American that I'm too close and too critical of their (our) strategies of distance and acceptance. When I see a FB post laughing at Trump, or horrified at Trump, I don't feel inspired. I see guilt, born of an unacknowledged regret for what's been built. You've made this. I've made this. We've gathered facts, produced information, formed knowledge against others. That's what we do well. I don't see the *will* to sacrifice what we've possessed and become possessed by. *Care* has been replaced by an image of concern. We brand ourselves on this *appearance*—the hashtag and the meme— by naming identities rather than caring for each other.

The fault lies not in "us" as individuals, but we must reckon with our participation, our making of this world. The conditions of oppression, historical as they are, are outside each of us; and yet there seems to be little reckoning about how each of us maintains such conditions.

Americans are not living, they're surviving, biding time until he's gone. That's what this impeachment is about. It's about removing the image that we've produced together through our consumption, our habits, and the comforts of security.

22 September, Kaohsiung

How we treat others is evident in how we deal with the lint guard on a laundry dryer. If it's a public machine, I don't remove the lint from the lint guard when I'm done with my load. Nor does anyone else for me and I don't expect it. But if I'm doing laundry at home and I live with my significant other, or if I'm at a relative's house doing laundry, I'll remove the lint when I'm done.

We care about what is close because love and consequences are localized phenomena. The politics of the lint guard. We expect too much in asking people to care about categories or identities that are not close to them.

29 September, Kaohsiung

What will we do when the plants go on strike? Or the cells? Or the genes? All of the living networks that will adapt to the endless cycles of oppression that collectively becomes 'the environment'—the smoke that fills the air, the toxins in the soil, the noise of politics filling every thought that resonates in affectations that permeate such networks like mist—will they learn absurdity, futility, and give up?

10 October, Kaohsiung

> "I think what's complicated for a lot of critics is that they are not naturally artistic people."[24]

Chuck Klosterman said this, just sort of vamping, in a discussion with Bill Simmons about the *Joker* movie. Bill and I both laughed when he said it. To me this hits on a great deal of the discourse of *Das Man*, idle talk, whatever one wishes to call it. There are so many critical people out there with blogs and twitter accounts and columns for all these post-Salon type corporate-owned websites. Movie and music critics today are well trained in critical theory, but they don't seem to care much for art. They function today in the correctional binary of condemnation or approval. They find an artistic expression and judge it as morally or ethically valuable or harmful based upon their criteria for right and wrong in society. They have their own standards and their own discourse. This is how all industries function. Every institution has its language.

Artists work differently. They are trying to create for an audience a viewpoint, scenario, set of conditions, environment, mood in which the expression can most fruitfully take flight. With a particular space and time of expression, we can feel how and why such expressions are expressed. *Joker* isn't a celebration of violence. There's no moral judgment or agenda at work. (That's the thinking of a critic.) Rather, the film is an attempt to bring people close to a

---

[24] See Episode 576 of *The Bill Simmons Podcast*, airdate: Oct. 2, 2019.

particular experience, to imagine how our very *milieu*, our close environment of relations, creates possible conditions for violence.

In other words, the critic (who speaks the *explicit* language of approval and condemnation) identifies the individual for what he has done. Trump is the obvious example here. The artist (who works in *implicit* gestures of expression) shows what is real through fictional scenarios (Trumpism). One lives on the outside, judges from the outside, using a particular language that always reasons from the distance of analysis and judgment. The other lives inside, working through emotions, affections and ineffable relations to let the one who experiences the art imagine a new thought and run with it.

In our current economics of digital content production, we have way more critics than artists. Art, and those who make it, must be defended.

12 October, Kaohsiung

"But the message of the pathway speaks just so long as there are men (born in its breeze) who can hear it. They are hearers of their origin, not servants of their production. In vain does man try with his plans to bring order to his globe if he does not order himself to the message of the pathway. The danger looms that today's men are hard of hearing towards its language. They have ears only for the noise of media, which they consider to be almost the voice of God. So man becomes distracted and path-less. The Simple seems monotonous to the distracted. The monotonous brings weariness. The annoyed find only the uniform. The Simple has fled. Its quiet power is exhausted."

- Martin Heidegger[25]

[25] *Martin Heidegger: Philosophical and Political Writings* (2003, Continuum).

This passage, beautifully stated, spoke to me today, expressing some genuine wisdom. Yet the more I read Heidegger the more he fades for me as someone I want to cite to support what I'm writing. There's a very real struggle I'm having of a Heidegger-Han-Kierkegaard "the way" conservatism and Bergson-Deleuze-Blanchot open future.

Still, Kierkegaard remains the exception; his radical faith being such a singular act of fortitude toward the impossible, in defiance of the dogmas of the day. That push is more aligned with Deleuze in this regard than Heidegger.

If you read Heidegger closely, not just here but in his full *oeuvre*, there is an appeal to obey that which has been forgotten. Great. But what is that? Is there one way? Because I think there is a pedestrian version of this in what the masses accept today—that there is a correct way of doing things, of acting, a Hellenistic *logos* that has in modernity lost its *account*. It's as true for the atheist as for the Christian. One possesses certainty over what *is* and only from this one takes action in accord with that certainty. Then there are the more postmodern leanings, the plurality of interpretation that allows for the openness of creative movement, of *different* thinking—directions and indications that produce, rather than follow, a path. But where does this lead if no one follows? Heidegger longs for the arrival, in listening, of forgotten authenticity. Taken to extremes he opens to the perversion of fascism. Deleuze invites the creativity of new thinking; but without a sense of belonging, one is left alone, exposed to the empty threads of nihilism.

I dwell on this a lot. And as I move now to Bataille, it seems he is getting at this very distinction. To me, it's the most important political question of our time. Is there a correct way to believe, and should our effort be to bring everyone else along? This is the approach of centrist liberalism, all the little critics in chorus with the major dogmas—progressive correctness equal *in strategy* to conservative correctness. It is a belief that there is something undeniably true, something that transcends this time of struggle. All we need to do is hear it. It is the church of *media*—all neon lights, high ceilings and right angles. It's a frenzied, noisy house of discord, levying blame and judgment that echoes across the rafters. It's a house built upon a lie of open discourse, reinforced through beams of commerce, careerism and corporatism. There is no listening here. This house of being lacks the authenticity Heidegger strives for.

Or are we to believe in the yet unimagined (see again: Hong Kong), not a return but a fragmentation into possibilities, to futures uncertain and unseen? A belief in the freedom of expressions (the plural is important). Here is a listening that does not obey and instead invents. The problem is, because it has no church it lacks a medium of listening.

All this is another way of saying that media has *replaced* thinking. Philosophy is no longer practiced. It has been replaced by mediated criticism. There is no need for philosophy when media does our core thinking for us, and at this core is making us believe we are thinking independent of it. This myth of transparency is its unspoken first commandment. In the speed of media-thought, no one has time for philosophy's thinking, which thinks in lingering silence. This is Byung-Chul Han's extended critique as well: at today's speed nothing holds, thought has no time to gather. Instead we have information, which gathers thought for us. It is the one critique that is shared among all the writers I mentioned above. Thought that needs to be thought has no time for thinking.

18 October, Kaohsiung

One could argue that the Overlook Hotel is a setting who functions as a character. One could then make the further argument that this character-setting functions as an allegory for, say, white supremacy, or patriarchy, or Foucauldian discipline—conditions that give rise to invisible systems of control. *The Shining* is not a film about Jack going mad. (Just as USA politics today is not a story about a madman in the White House.) It's a film about an impossibly complex, interweaving, immanent and transcendental mesh of matter and spirit gathered in a particular time and space in which one small family comes to find itself. Each of these three human characters responds to this environment-character in different ways. These responses, these gatherings within this gathering—so very Stephen King and so very Stanley Kubrick—is what *The Shining* is about at the level of being-in-the-world. Any allegories beyond this are the stuff of cultural discourse.

FRAGMENTS 5: 2020

17 February, Seoul

The sobering reality of this virus is beginning to emerge.

It may turn out that this becomes a kind of normal, which means that the virus kills a lot of people but is not lethal enough to stop the mechanisms of global capitalism. At some point, I'm guessing a month or so, the gears of commerce are going to have to start moving again, quarantine will seem pointless, people will travel and go back to work, billions will get it and a million will die by Christmas.

It will come to define this year and probably far beyond that. (A vaccine won't be ready until well into 2021.) We'll stay home, watch a movie, those of us who have the privilege of making that choice. Public spaces and events will become barren and ignored. Live music, theaters, sporting events, restaurants, classrooms: we'll livestream it. "Let's just stay in." will become a common phrase.

Another shock, like the politics of today, will become everyday conversation as we hide in fear because we're able to. Those with good health and good care and coverage will be okay, while those without will die. We'll be so inundated with news of deaths of poor people in poor areas of the world that it will stop being news.

Every once in a while, we'll remember to talk about it in our apartments and houses over dinner. We'll comfort ourselves in the necessity of population reduction and the benefits of reduced fuel consumption, a twin *deus ex machina* against ecological catastrophe.

All the while we'll remember to add the necessary coda:

"But isn't it sad, those people?"

"Yes, dear, it is."

12 March, Kaohsiung

Here are, straight from the gut and fueled by an afternoon coffee, ten things I *think* I think about this coronavirus:

1. This is <u>not just about a virus</u>. There is the virus, a health issue. There is the public response to the virus, a civil issue. There is the fear/anxiety/disregard of/about the virus, an existential issue. All of these are in play. But there is also...

2. The <u>governmental response</u> to the virus, revealing passive expressions of nationalistic posturing. This to me is revealing interesting traits about various nations that I know something about at least a little bit. China: History is long and this is just one of those things that kinda happened but we did what we do well and shut everything down and it's not our problem anymore and by the way we're going to return the insult and start quarantining *you* now. Taiwan: See! We're not the mainland! Korea: Big data is a good thing. (And whatever there is to be said about that—see No. 8 below—it's also true that they've been admirable in their response and are way ahead of the curve, as is Taiwan.) Thailand: Please come back. Japan: Nothing to see here. Europe: We're

totally fucked but we're on it! USA: We're totally fine and we're totally not on it at all because it's not our fault and how's the stock market today?

3. This virus is going to put into question the whole <u>legitimacy of open societies</u>. The States prides itself on rugged individualism. This is not going to work in this situation. You need a strong government that people believe in and you need to step back and trust them to take care of shit. US citizens since Reagan are terrible at this. People in the States will recognize that the West failed compared to Asia because of how Asian nations are able to respond in a way that the States cannot. Political dumbfuckery will mutate in the coming weeks and Americans are going to flip the fuck out.

4. Banking off of No. 3, this is not a good time if your government works under a profit-based system of health care. The <u>United States system of health coverage</u> is not equipped to implement the *preventative* measures needed for a situation like this. We will see whether the States are equipped in terms of hospitalization, beds and ventilators and the like for those already sick. But what is needed at a level of curtailment is free and readily available testing. Alas, the ship has sailed on Covid-19, but it should be considered for the next virus sure to come.

5. I've lived through three life-altering, the-world-will-never-be-the same shifts: 1) the digital/internet emergence, 2) 9/11, 3) Covid-19. The first was a slow movement with no single event, the second and third are stunners. This one is more of a slow realization than a sudden shock, although it seems shock is there. This will <u>completely alter the global economy</u>. Everything is going to move to screens, entire industries will fold, online education will become the norm, travel as an industry will never be the same, and at least for the present, racism against Asians will

become commonplace and will move to the front of the cultural conversation for years to come.

6. This is my way-too-soon-for-this comment but I'll let it fly: <u>This is going to help the planet</u>. In fact, it might be just what the planet needs, if you set aside for a moment the very real human suffering, sadness and misery. No one's ready to say this publicly, but it's true. Aging population problem? Curtailed. Ecological disaster? Perhaps averted (reduced fuel emissions, travel, overall consumption, etc.). Runaway capitalism? Cancel everything and let all these luxury industries suffer and die. Maybe the aquarium theory—the idea that when the planet needs saving, some higher power nudges the rocks in the tank to avert disaster—is real. I wonder, though, about problems of migration, loss of environmental regulations, who knows what other unknown breed of chaos... I don't mean to be cold. A lot of old and sick people will die and that is horrible. But it's also probably true that in an epochal sense, bloated consumption, free-wheeling travel, people moving around everywhere, and economic privilege of this magnitude could not sustain itself. We have been directly confronting unprecedented ecological destruction, so this aspect cannot be ignored.

7. Beware of <u>states of exception</u>. You're going to be hearing a lot of them. "Times are different, so you need to do X." This will come up in your job, in political discourse, in media, in advertising, in fear-mongering of various kinds, in what someone above you is telling you is the best for everyone during these extraordinary circumstances. Power loves situations like these. It's like power is its own virus, seeking to infect and control those it can through soulless vampires (be they people or whole institutions) looking to capitalize. I'm not saying to resist everything, but try to recognize when the exception is authentic and when it is opportunistic.

8. Combining some of the points mentioned, we may be facing a future of two independent lines of acceleration: <u>ecological healing and automation</u>. As the planet breathes a little easier over the course of a year or two, automation will expand. What we're learning from South Korea and Taiwan is that Big Data—purchase tracking, record keeping, the storing of personal information, tracing movements, etc.—is the solution to future coronavirus outbreaks. What may be good for the planet, and good for controlling runaway virus threats to people, will be bad for privacy, freedom of expression, and freedom from institutional machinery.

9. <u>Do not make fun of this virus</u>. Just ask Rudy Gobert and Matt Gaetz.

10. <u>Joe Biden will be the next US president</u>. I say this not as a hope. I am convinced that Bernie Sanders' economic platform is far better equipped for this and future outbreaks. Rather, I predict this because 1) Trump supporters' F-you attitude will deflate as older people start to die and as they personally face a real crisis that he's clearly inept at handling; 2) Democrats will lazily appeal to a pre-existing belief in Biden as the "safe" choice rather than shifting toward the best choice in Bernie. Once Biden is the nominee, we're looking at a historic landslide. Of course, as things change, this could also change. But if it's not Biden, a Bernie presidency is far more likely than a second Trump term.

14 March, Kaohsiung

Online education is already starting to become complicated by problems. Three points are important to creatively problematize this situation:

1. Always serve the <u>interests of students</u> above that of the institution. This is what I meant by "beware of states of exception" before. The institution wants you to move your teaching online so that during "normal" times it can be monitored, quantified, automated and duplicated, removing the student-teacher relationship from the equation and threatening the intellectual rights of the teacher. This situation is just one example of how higher education is becoming corporatized.

2. The more video you record for classes, the more you become a YouTuber and you contribute to the <u>YouTube-ification of higher education</u>. I tell my students on the first day of every class: "You could easily go to YouTube and learn what I'm teaching you. What is different about the university is that we are together engaged in discussion, learning how to apply theoretical concepts toward practice." Perhaps this is a myth in 2020, but I want to believe it's still the case. We have a young generation now who hates school and believes they know everything from watching YouTube. Online learning legitimizes this attitude. I'll do everything I can to fight it, to preserve confrontational and present discussion-based learning in the classroom.

3. Students already spend too much time <u>staring at screens</u>. Education should remain a rare opportunity to be present and engaged in a live community of shared expression. My online approach therefore is to livestream the class and record nothing. Although they're staring at screens, at least they participate *in real time*.

20 March, Kaohsiung

If this is the end of days, it's just the worst apocalypse imaginable. No heroes, no battles, no narratives. Yet it's somehow tragically appropriate: everyone separated from each other—the other as carrier—hiding inside homes. Netflix unto death.

I get the practicality, the logic. Minds today have developed exceptional capacities for doing what makes perfect sense. But if this is dying, it sure isn't living.

This preservation of "bare life" above living is what Giorgio Agamben is warning us about.[26] But also... assuming this is not the end, the "state of exception" we're willing to foster raises questions not only of what we're doing right now, but of what comes after this.

This is philosophy's value against the myopic disciplines of science. It's not about what happened but what happens next. We're going to have to ask ourselves how we wish to live.

*****

I'm fine here in Kaohsiung. We just had a little spike in cases, but the government has been so Jedi in closing off the island that we've been spared. People walk around freely, no talk of distancing. I'm fortunate to be here in a place of stellar healthcare, just in case. I have masks and sanitizer and toilet paper (I still don't get the TP thing America). Every morning someone points a temperature gun to my forehead and I'm a consistent 36.6. I get a stamp on my hand, say thanks, and I'm off to my office or to class.

---

[26] See https://itself.blog/2020/03/17/giorgio-agamben-clarifications/.

Underneath it all, I also feel quite sad and isolated, and if my mind wanders, trapped. A couple of days ago, the Taiwan government announced that no foreigners are allowed into the country unless they have an ID card or are willing to undergo the stringent two-week quarantine period. This means that I'm separated from the woman I love, and we hate this fact. Time is moving exceedingly slow and a feeling of bliss and hope for the future with her is infused with a sadness that pervades everything. At this ineffable existential level, I fear the now and the next. I can only hope that staying focused on projects will help the time pass into better days. Love will find a way.

30 March, Kaohsiung

Harmony is the *mimesis* of melody into another line, a demiurgical crafting of the unconscious against and alongside the conscious thought—a Dionysian subtext, the binding of *another* to the graceful voice of Apollo.

*****

I do believe that in the end, there will be only music.

2 April, Kaohsiung

I'll say it again, this apocalypse is utterly uninspiring. There's nothing cinematic about it, nothing narrative. The metaphors are so lifeless that there's no allegory to shape into form. There will be "stories" when this passes, but they will be uninteresting. We'll tell of the horrors, the sacrifices, being separated from homes and loved ones. Domestic violence is a real thing; racism against Asians will grow. But imagine green-lighting such stories. Domestic violence with a couple sitting at home, mostly staring at computers and TV screens. Racism typed over computer screens, hate crimes taking place on a brief walk as a break from otherwise staying at home, surviving, staring at screen technology. Where's a movie script in that?

The problem with this fight is there's no fight. This is because there's no conflict. Conflict is the lifeblood of a good yarn. Conflict comes from someone facing a choice, being forced to make a decision. It doesn't happen over a mobile phone, it happens at places, in situations and within environments, through a collision of events.

Sitting at home is not a fight. It's not a struggle. There's no story because there's no lived conflict. Nothing is worth filming. It's only hard. There is no cycle of bad choices, mistakes, learning, confronting. There's no migration, no travel, no change of setting. Character development is non-existent because there's nothing to face, nothing to overcome. Growth happens when someone acts, makes a decision, moves one's body. But in this, progress is inert and passive. The Science State tells us what to do and we do it. Victories happen when another day passes without getting sick. All events are negations of activity; no decision, no choice. We wait.

The real-life heroes are the doctors and nurses. But even there, what are the arcs being formed? An endless stream of ICU patients, repetitions of the same. A patient comes into a hospital and lies in a hospital bed. If the patient improves that patient leaves. If not, that patient goes into ICU and is (if lucky) put on a ventilator until recovery or death. It's an inert battle. Each person is undifferentiated, converted into the data of demographics.

This is what happens when people become carriers. What is the other in the existential crisis of Covid-19? The other is a potential host, a carrier of disease, a sack of biology. But there's no threat here. One either is or is not. So we stay away. The viral movement between carriers has no "inciting incident." There's no zombie bite, nothing so eventful. Nothing happens. It just... happens. So we distance ourselves. We wait.

There are no protagonists because there are no antagonists. Even more absurd than Camus' plague, there is no point to the story. Functionally, the antagonist's role is to constantly usurp the protagonist's movement toward some goal. What is the goal in this story? What is to be overcome? The enemy is a virus. But it's not like a zombie virus in which we see some change, a tragic turn. This thing is entirely invisible. It has no face, no affection-image, no closeup. The threat is merely sad.

Covid-19 takes absurdity to its zenith. It is so absurd that there's no decision to be made, nothing to do, nothing to make. There's no difficult choice, no action to take.

But it's not without its irony. The irony is that it is our own particular hell that has come back to destroy us. We've nurtured a generation of people to stare passively at screens and wait to see some outcome or result from it. We let machines do our work, allow ourselves to be entertained by surfaces. We wait for downloads and automate our daily lives. The virus is a natural extension of this. People don't act, they let information move through them while they wait.

Even if the struggle had a narrative, the aesthetics are terrible. Stories come through rectangles. A person or a couple holds up a rectangle and reports being stranded on a cruise ship, quarantined in a room, taking a brief break on duty at a hospital. Someone pushes a red record button and we see bad photography— bulbous faces in wide-angle auto-settings, staring just off camera, speaking into bad microphones—tinny, desperate voices expressing their own personal horror, sadness or inconvenience.

We've also engineered the solutions through our consumer choices. The mobile phone was a luxury that became a necessity. As a necessity, it has become bound to its user and vice/versa. Success stories are tied to how well one is monitored in one's relations to other possible carriers. Morality lies in waiting, surviving, communicating and consuming. It's the perfect bad script.

10 April, Kaohsiung

After reading a brief piece written by my friend Jeremy,[27] I ask myself: What do we do when all we listen to is compressed renderings of digital voices and all we see are screens that reproduce the faded pixels of faces? We might save our lives, but at the risk of losing our souls. The sad irony of coronavirus: to save our bodies we have to abandon their reason for existing. We are all carriers, whether we have the virus or not. To the State, we simply carry our bodies. To ourselves, we fail to comprehend death to the point that we convince ourselves that it's okay to abandon life.

*****

Social media commentary lately has begun to shift. Now people instruct people about what to do and what not to do. One should vote one's conscience, or choose not to vote if that is how one feels. What disturbs me is the constant need to actively negate—this

---

[27] See https://positionspolitics.org/jeremy-fernando-on-living-in-the-age-of-pandemic/.

anything-but-evil course of action. I see very little that is positive, including Biden. But there is also the argument, which I'm sympathetic to, of a gesture of positive non-participation in a corrupt system. Voting itself can be viewed as unethical in that its participants, through participation, uphold a corrupt structure, particularly when the supposed good guys are continuing a pro-wealthy, pro-capitalist, pro-elitist, pro-hawkish agenda. If I vote for Biden and Biden wins, the system is legitimized and maintained—the pain of the working class, the continuance of wealth inequality, ecological destruction, etc. Such a vote, this gesture, runs counter to my sense of ethics. I prefer to express ethics in ways that are other than what *is*—not a negation, but the positive expression of not voting. As with Nietzsche: the no that is a yes.

12 May, Kaohsiung

I watch movies for the music they make.

I listen to music for the films I make.

15 May, Kaohsiung

There are no worldwide numbers on mortality data with the virus, but there are US state of New York demographics, regularly updated. Here are the mortality numbers as of 13 May:

- 75% had underlying conditions. 0.7% did not. (the other 24.3% = not known)

- 48.7% were over the age of 75. 4.5% were under the age of 44.

I know it's hard for people to accept, but most people (Americans anyway) care about what is local. We think at the level, in order, of individual, family, neighborhood, city, nation. Belief is produced by familiarity, repetition and habit. Information fragments this. It demands that we now, rationally, "care" about what is produced informationally. I'm not justifying people who don't want to wear masks, or who rush out to a bar when a lockdown is lifted. Because at the level of public good, these people are acting rashly and irresponsibly. I'm arguing that "care" occurs at the level of localized experience, and we've been highly trained to care in visual terms.

We are sensorial creatures who believe in our rational minds. But being reasonable about something invisible limits the imaginative capacity. This is why it's hard to "care" about information. We care about what we live. Empathy can't penetrate a screen. It's felt through experience. If we want to change the way people respond to the plight of others, to a collective engagement, we have to question the technology that has fragmented life into data. We have to question how education has driven young people toward the economic viability of technology, data and automation at the expense of non-economic virtues of the humanities, critical thinking and aesthetics. We have to fight against this liberal tendency to dismiss people who operate at the level of feelings and beliefs.

This is why I understand the desire to fight against lockdowns. It's not always because of a belief in some conspiracy, as is being painted. (Conspiracies are born of a feeling that lacks the ability to see.) It's because people want to live, in their community. I both admire and am repulsed by what Americans are doing. The actions are stupid, but that's the world America has built. I'm not willing to cast aside someone who acts absurdly when they live in an absurd world. At least it expresses *something*.

16 May, Kaohsiung

STATE: You are a sack of biology. Everything you are permitted and not permitted to do must be in service to The Economy.

CITIZEN: OK.

STATE: Occasionally I will say publicly that I care about your personal health. But really, I need you to stay alive to service The Economy.

CITIZEN: I understand.

STATE: Good. We'll get through this together. In the meantime, keep surviving. Consume things, watch the news, vote in elections, pay attention. We need you to continue your false hope in the great society to come.

CITIZEN: Fuck off.

STATE: What's that?

CITIZEN: Nothing, thank you Lord. We'll get through this together.

22 May, Kaohsiung

Americans seem to be really upset that the United States is behaving like the United States. Even Trump is a pretty normal product of USA Today. He is both the apex and nadir of a line of Americanism that has been fueled over the past couple of generations by the combustable proliferation and convergence of power, entertainment, identity and media technologies—that is, the world liberalism built.

The USA is grounded on a distrust of authority and power and a pragmatic path toward solutions and conclusions. All of the art, innovations and culture it produces come from this. At its best, it results in positive acts of resistance and progressivism, such as the Civil Rights movements, Occupy Wall Street, and Black Lives Matter. It's very difficult to suddenly demand that a cultural psychology be different from what it has always been, which is to distrust and think as an individual against the commun(al)ism of the collective. Sometimes people come together when an enemy is visibly present. But that's not this. This is a moment in history when individualism and free thinking does not work because we have been educating the wrong things in schools, because government across the board is composed of distrustful leaders, and because we are intolerant of what lives in abstraction.

Americans have a strong sense of resistance against doing what everyone else does. This is a valuable trait. Doubt is the core of critical thinking. It's been amplified by terrible public leadership, media proliferation, dismissal of spirit, and poor education. But just as awful are the universal moralists, the puritans who demand that everyone act the same way. It brings to mind *The Invasion of the Body Snatchers*, that great B-movie from 1956, released at the height of the Red Scare. There's no Red Scare here, rather a different cultural battle: the meeting of the universal and the individual. Like any philosophical problem, questions don't lead to easy answers. But all Americans would do well to pause a moment and consider that the hyperbolic, conspiracy theorist, non-mask-wearing caricature of individualism, and the kowtowing and condescending rationalist who believes everything corporate media sells, are both grown in the same garden of education, government and media.

Everyone has reason; at least, everyone believes oneself to be practicing rationalism. But every person is also composed of habits, impressions and beliefs fostered by parenting, information, suppressed traumas, fragmented recollections, and displaced feelings that constantly infect any rational practice. You're not a scientist, you read language that is filtered by interpretation, research grants, myopic reporting, advertising revenues and corporate agendas. Voting, commerce and taxation by every member of the public continues all of this.

If you don't like the idiots around you, consider how you're ingesting the world that renders people as unidimensional; consider turning yourself toward the social conditions themselves that have given rise to shared problems.

30 May, Kaohsiung

I had all these things I wanted to get done on my Saturday, but I can't pull myself away from what's happening in Minneapolis. The discourse around this just deepens my despair. Not in the passion and the outrage, but in the *telos* that is drawn. Derek Chauvin killed George Floyd, brutally, on camera. Oppressed people felt it, deeper than I'll ever know, and responded as they should, by taking to the streets, destroying and stealing material wealth denied to them. The president responded with names and death threats.

That's what happened. But that's not what's happening. I wonder if people will be pacified by Chauvin going to jail and Trump being voted out of office in the fall. It seems this is the middle-class, white American *telos*. It's a *telos* born of a guilt-ridden America that has replaced God with Law as the arbiter of justice and the holy punishment of individual illegalities. It's picking a dandelion from a field of dandelions and hoping that a green field will magically appear tomorrow. Or perhaps we don't care. *Telos* is closure, and the murmur of white America seems placated with closure for themselves and their own guilty consciences.

The incident is the incident. But the condition is the problem. The problem cannot end at racists. It has to address the realities of white supremacy, which is a condition shared by all Americans.

Eddie S. Glaude Jr. asked on PBS' The News Hour broadcast today:

"How does one live in such a time? Here we are in a moment in which we're dealing with a global pandemic, trying to figure out how to live under these conditions. And we still have to deal with the fact that our children and our family members and our friends can be killed by the police. ... I don't think we can wait on those who are invested in an idea of whiteness to change. If we do that, we're gonna lose another generation. ... Those of us who have learned the lessons of our history, those who want to imagine America differently, we have to start building a world where those kinds of beliefs have no quarter to breathe. ... We need to change the way in which police see black men and women, which is rooted in a deep cultural ethos. We need to address the fundamental, underlying conditions of resource-deprived communities where people don't have a living wage, where they don't have a decent education, where they don't have decent housing. All of this is rooted in this belief that America is a white nation. If we have to wait on those folks who are committed to that, America will continue to be this ugly place. So I believe, in my heart of hearts, that you and I and those of us who are committed to a more just America, a new America, we have to get about the business of building it. Now. Covid has changed everything. We can't go back to what was. We can't allow people to double down on their ugly commitments. We have to finally muster the courage to build a new America, or this thing will go to hell."[28]

The *telos* needs to widen into something far more fertile. We can't be done with incidents. We cannot take a pill for this. The way to widen is to embrace the creation of new worlds, to give birth to

---

[28] A transcript of this broadcast can be retrieved at https://www.pbs.org/newshour/show/how-response-to-george-floyds-death-reflects-accumulated-grievance-of-black-america.

new practices of thinking, believing, communing and legislating from out of this dying world we have now. We don't need to heal. We need to be reborn.

14 June, Kaohsiung

"Conspiracy theory" and "fake news" are ideas that arise from a drive for inquiry tainted by a flawed method of inquiry. Or put another way, ...from a virtue of doubt that lacks an authentic path to explore the validity of other possibilities. The psychological problem is framed as a practice of willful ignorance based on faith. Against this error is proposed the virtue of reason, which thinks critically and leads to rigorous conclusions. But this is myopic. Ignorance, as Socrates said, is a virtue. Reason, as Freud said, is flawed. The medium between requires a kind of language that helps to navigate the anxiety that threatens to land upon flawed conclusions. Thought benefits from concepts that act as guides, bubbles of inspiration if you will, that maintain the necessity of questioning. It also benefits from a nurturing of doubt and avoiding a kind of psychosis brought about by a bombardment of statements.

Another way of putting this is that thought requires thinking. The *kind of language* that one integrates guides thought to its destinations. The medium of language in today's politics, cultural struggles and bioethics is the internet. We are in turn mediated by it, *becoming* it. This is exacerbated in situations of confinement and isolation from others in physical proximity. We are awash in information, images and statements that arrange into codes, directives of thinking. Usually these are driven by capitalist institutions that thrive on discipline, knowledge, and other structures of control and production. The statements that result swim with our nonlinguistic affective relations—beliefs, feelings, imagination, memory, intuitions—that guide, color and harden into the language one has. Experience is multiple. It is organic, technological, informational, linguistic and visual. Thought is the arrangement of and from this multiplicity. Within the noise of the milieu, one notices and arranges a stream into listening; one obeys the stream that makes the most "sense" and says "I hear." It is an exercise both active and passive.

It is tempting to identify the problem as one of education. But that word conjures further problematics of power and systemic programming. In so many situations, education is the spark of rebellion, particularly in younger generations. Solutions to how we think would have to lie at criticizing the dominance of techno-capitalist proliferation, the systems and directives of thinking, structures of self-surveillance, peer pressures, language correction, and other ceaseless streams of judgment. We should celebrate the human desire that falls into the traps of conspiracy and fakery, but instead we demonize their inquiries, forgetting that the infrastructure encourages a knowing ignorance across all levels of thought competency. Worse than the conspiracist is the one unwilling to doubt.

*****

We are deciding now who is "essential" and who is "nonessential." Grocery workers and nurses are essential, artists are nonessential.

When you read the history of Greek and Chinese cultures, you find that art and storytelling were not only what people did, nor were they simply serving a morally didactic function; they actually (as scholarship suggests) are what produced the civil structures of society. Laws, morals and community came only after art and stories; storytelling and art functioned as the production of community, morals and law. Dance and music in particular are the forms that bound people together, moving from chaos to village, from which followed a culture and a society.

Is that just history then, something to dismiss as the past? What happens when art is isolated and privately streamed? Netflix, Hulu, HBO, popular movies, popular music, books. Today, they remind us of the communal ethics now lost.

11 August, Kaohsiung

Reading William James 1...

"we remember our own theories, our own discoveries, combinations, inventions, in short whatever 'ideas' originate in our own brain, a thousand times better than exactly similar things which are communicated to us from without."[29]

William James keeps reminding me what a task it would be to try to change the minds of others who have lived experiences different than one's own. Each of us is a world of experience, learning, hurt, fear, interest, joy, belief and fascination. What one gives care to is what is most interesting and vivid to one's etchings of belief and conviction. Yet we abuse ourselves with constant complaints about the fact that others do not share our own world of thought and experience. An impossible, Sisyphean task.

---

[29] William James, *The Principles of Psychology Volume One* (1950, Dover).

Each life is its own world, shared and exchanged with other worlds. But the exchange is polluted by technical precision; we don't feel the other so much anymore. Instead we read their lines of text. We listen though microphones that have been granted to people in power, thereby granting them an image of authority. Technology has given us the power to reproduce the authority of forms. We've become very good at this. And now we're all casters: newscasters, science-casters, opinion-casters, fact-casters, reason-casters.

We've had variations of this throughout history. Before philosophy there were real magicians. Their magic was the statement, the suggestion. They wandered the streets using a power called poetry. They arranged words in strange combinations to cast spells on the people they met, who would stop in their tracks if the spell was arranged in such a way to produce something earth-shattering. We're not so amazed anymore, not while we're awash in casting that is only allowed to be explicit in its goals. No one is mystified, the poetics is lost. We are reproducers of data without the intimacy of encounters.

Elenchus, the Socratic method, doesn't work anymore, not in a world without sensation, without an immediate physical response, without seeing the eyes and hearing the timbre of the other. We thought communication was the answer, but it's clear that this was wrong. If we want to change ourselves, we need to change how we—all of us together in so many different possible ways—experience the world. How are we learning? How are we thinking? How much are we willing to let others into the sphere of learning and experiencing? We'd have to give up our pleasure in the sport of dismissing types and casting names, casting accusations, casting blame. Once the joy of this game is gone, the vitriolic, toxic response dies too.

14 August, Kaohsiung

Reading William James 2...

In his chapter on reasoning in *The Principles of Psychology*, James has a subsection on "modes of conceiving." I'll spare the technical matters and put it this way: When we aim to conceive what something is, we take something as its essence and attribute it as fact. But for James, each thing (object, event, person, incident, whatever) has multiple essences and multiple properties. So when we conceive fact through essence, "We mutilate the fullness of reality." To have all knowledge we'd have to conceive all relations. But in our reasoning, we think in single lines. We take one relation, which forms one of its attributes, one angle to conceive, ignoring the others. We commonly do this: I single out one side of a person or thing that has some bearing on me, and in such a situation, I reason a conclusion, ignoring other attributes. No property can encapsulate the whole. Time is also a key element to these processes: circumstances constantly change. Nevertheless, we are driven to class something by name, and in so doing we are necessarily "unjust" to all other aspects. My thinking is for the sake of my doing and I can only do this one thing right now.

Another way of saying this is that we think of the "fact" as "essence" based upon a single property born of need, interest or desire (James' American pragmatism fully evident here). Not only are there other facts to a whole, there are also other essences. To know the entirety of this thing we would have to know not only all facts but also all essences, and to accomplish this we'd have to follow all the attributes born of all the relations it is engaged in during this moment, a moment which is different from yesterday and will be different tomorrow.

While we live differences, we work from identities. We class something under a name presuming that this name is the essence of that thing. We essentialize according to (in James' terms) our subjective needs and interests. Second, we hear a lot about "following the science" with an overtly religious fervor. Following the science may be good for narrow reproducibility—science only thinks science —but we take it as truth. In the process, we strip away the larger possible awareness of this vast network of other facts, essences, relations and circumstances that must be necessarily ignored for such a following to occur.

Skeptical people feel this intuitively. But such emergent paths of doubt are flawed as well, because whereas science is narrowed to what it can observe under the limits of its own method and parameters of study, skepticism follows paths of, according to James, need, vividness, desire, interest, repetition, habit and attractiveness. Both science and human doubt follow habitual and repetitive processes. Both are grounded on training, learning and interest. But in the process of concluding, which to James is the driving impetus of understanding, we have abandoned far more than we have gathered. Doubt follows a path of desire and interest; science follows a model of reproduction and isolation. Neither comes close to accounting for the varieties of experience in any complicated situation that we then name under the container of fact or truth. And as James implies elsewhere, all this reproduction limits us. In such narrowness, we lose the ability for production, which is the realm of creative thinking, poetry, art, etc.

It's also important to underscore that for James, all this occurs both at the inner subjective level and the outer objective level. The reason I suspect that we value science over productive thought is that we fully recognize and admit that thought is flawed; but we have total faith that the instruments of ascertaining nature are now more reliable than productively thinking nature. This outside-of-thinking aspect—this faith—used to be reserved for God. Indeed, thought of

God is supposed to save us from the threats of nature. But in a post-God liberalism, science is the new ground of sanity in the war against nature, life and chaos. We push aside the possibility of productive knowing for a more secure reproduction of what institutions and experts already know. This is pragmatic, religious and dangerous.

16 August, Kaohsiung

Reading William James 3...

Today brings to an end my five-or-so weeks studying William James' *The Principles of Psychology*—the "long course" as it's called. I read about 1,200 of the 1,400 or so pages, skipping over the stuff that felt dated. Isolated, chronically bored, and compulsive by habit, I compiled 120 pages of notes and then wrote a 33-page lit review.

It's not my first time with James. I read his *Varieties of Religious Experience, A Pluralistic Universe*, and *Essays in Radical Empiricism*, plus a few other essays, for my dissertation. I enjoy the clarity of his writing, the rebelliousness of his concepts (what a thinker is supposed to do), and the beautiful way he's able to express the otherness of thinking—the all-too-real fringes of thought and experience that get lost as we constantly endeavor to take control of our minds within the impossible complexity of ever-shifting experience.

My takeaways from this experience are far too numerous to mention. But if I had to choose one, it's that as with Freud, we have no idea what we're doing when we think we're doing exactly what we think we know we're doing. Freud to me is a practitioner of narrowing—on particular neuroses, traumas, the unconscious, dreams, symbols and language. James is an advocate of expansion—

broadening back out to critique how philosophy and science have ignored sensation, belief and spirit. It's too easy to say James was the mystic and Freud was the analyst. James was a real scientist who followed and responded to the medical research of his time and produced lasting philosophical concepts from it.

If I have a criticism of James it's that he's very... American. By that I mean the pragmatism that we now live in was clearly a product of his ideas. There is tremendous emphasis given in his writing to ends, goals, even things like property and material acquisition. But when he does this, it's not a virtue but a diagnosis. He's right. We (Americans) tend to photograph the image of the goal before we live the moments. In doing so, we've lost a sense of the wider conditions of experience, and the far more numerous fringes of reality that get cast aside in targeted thinking. In this, I found myself nodding often as I reflected on the current state of American socio-political thought.

We shouldn't beat ourselves up for this. Rather it's helpful, even ethical, to acknowledge that what interests every person is that which is most interesting and beneficial to that person. This is the empirical fact of the mind doing what it needs to do. In addition to this interest, other processes hide and emerge as fringes and resonances, things like empathy and altruism. These can't be forced on another mind; they need to be given space to breathe, to be nurtured so they can become like grooves on a record, a melody that plays.

21 August, Kaohsiung

Seeing is perceptual; hearing is imaginative. One presents; the other makes.

28 August, Kaohsiung

Byung-Chul Han makes an observation in *Good Entertainment* that is obvious but which I never fully gave thought to. Regarding the blurring of entertainment with news, information and education in today's consciousness, he writes of "the similarity of the external frame" in all of it.[30] And it made me think, well yeah: We go to the same rectangular surface—a desensitized oracle of the narrow gaze—to absorb both news and entertainment. It's been this way since the 1950s with the personal family television sets. Then the computer came, but it was separated from the TV, the phone and the movie screen. With today's realization of "convergence"—another "revolution" pioneered by 1990s corporate startup weasels—we now go to the same screen for news, information, knowledge, communication, TV, movies, sports, violent games, porn, even love. Coming as they do through the same rectangle, it's no surprise that our view of the world consists of recombinations of these categories of form that become taken as real experience.

Han wrote *Good Entertainment* in 2016. Let's bring this up to 2020. First, Trump is not an anomaly but a natural product of the ecosystem we have celebrated through our grand advances in technology. Important issues of gender and race equality come in explosions of screened, rectangular representations. It exposes wounds, but encourages passive observation, even fascination, of them, like watching a movie. And in a year of lockdowns, border closures, and "stay at home" orders (BLM protests and lockdowns alike), we consult the screen passively for all our information, news, entertainment and communication, and then respond through the same passive screen. This response, this reactivity, offers the illusion

---

[30] All references here to Byung-Chul Han are: *Good Entertainment* (2019, MIT Press).

of activity, a participation that one knows is being observed and judged.

What's also changed this year is that education and intimate relations now stream through the same frame. The move to online education, internet dating, and screened togetherness has been going for a while. But it's now a daily requirement, not ancillary or a means but a substitute, a phantom. Teaching and learning are seen and acted out through the news/entertainment screen. All of it is a 2D surface masquerading as lived. Lovers separated share the same screen—a connection without intimacy, or perhaps with a performance of intimacy, screened as it is.

It's all okay though because it's temporary, they say. But it's not temporary, and it's not okay. This is how states of exception function. The mind adapts to the exception and the norms of social order maintain what worked as what is working. And what works is not life. What works is the imposition of order, predictability, commodity and discipline that is accepted by the citizens who advance it.

9 September, Kaohsiung

Nothing is the same as it was before.

Every day begins in a state of illusion.

Sameness is a means of organization, a psychosomatic attachment to habits and activities that we repeat.

We wake in the morning to the same bedroom. But the self, the bedroom and the moment are all different. To attend to this difference, one would have to become aware to waking to a new day and a new self.

Sameness is what one commonly adheres to for continuity and identity.

Difference manifests in real repetitions.

Only difference truly repeats.

20 September, Kaohsiung

I've been doing a second reading of Deleuze's *Nietzsche and Philosophy*. Now under the influence of William James, I find myself thinking of James quite a lot in Deleuze's exposition. I think this is because Deleuze is drawing out the psychologist element of Nietzsche. It is a non-Freudian psychology, a psychology of the body, of habit and memory, of multiplicity, pluralism and resonance, of active and reactive forces. All of these are meeting points of Nietzsche and James.

This again gives rise to the question of why Deleuze ignored James in his own writings (except for his book on Leibniz). I suspect it's because Deleuze wanted to emphasize the external rather than the internal. All three thinkers were consumed by the possibilities of thinking, and that thinking is an "actual" activity (that is, a real actualization). But Deleuze's psychology is far more interested in situating thinking within a wide range of other, more external, actualizing processes, rather than the internalized habits, grooves and streams of James.

James the pragmatist describes how we come to our ends. Deleuze the Nietzschean is instead doing the work of ethics and virtue. He wanted to emphasize how we break these patterns, how consciousness is capable of creating its own spillways that diverge from the stream, something James did not do much. James the diagnostician, Deleuze and Nietzsche the antagonizers of joyful creation.

23 September, Kaohsiung

The recent documentary *The Social Dilemma* is getting a lot of attention on my socially mediated knowledge streams. Much of the commentary attends to the idea of social media as a drug. But we can't repeat the errors of the 1980s, when we condemned and shamed "crackheads," ignoring the institutional racism that produced the problem. This "drug" cannot be narrowed to the individual psyche and its recreational consumption and self-abuse. This drug is prescribed and educated by all the various institutions that advance opportunities for the young, in particular. In this, social media is pushed and peddled not on street corners and back alleys, but by grade schools, universities and businesses. It is not recreational, it is a necessity. To survive economically, to have a career, one must adopt, nurture and habituate these forms. It's an imperative, a mandate. Our institutions of learning and business push people toward harmful, habitual drug consumption.

Watching the film also made me think more about the generational gap, how 50-year-olds like me use these drugs compared to 20- and 30-year-olds. I think one major difference is quite simple:

The period.

A couple of years ago, a younger friend of mine told me that she thought I was angry with her because I ended a text message with a period. I didn't understand how she came to this conclusion. But I've recently noticed how younger people don't use periods in text messages whereas I do. I've asked people about this and I've been told that the period can be taken as a sign of aggression.

My old mind doesn't understand this. A period is how one ends a sentence. How is that aggressive? Thinking back now, I recognize that this is a different era, and digital technology is ageist at its core. It feeds off the young. This brings a different question, that of addiction: Without periods, with a steady stream of lines and fragments, how does one know when the thought is over? When does the exchange, the conversation, end? It seems that this open sending is designed to encourage a continuous exchange.

And then it hits me: Maybe this is why my students can't stop staring into the goddamned rectangle—the conversation never ends. This practice to me is anxiety-inducing—the not-knowing when I'm allowed to conclude the exchange. When do I get to put this crack pipe down and go back to living in the world of genuine sensual experience?

I'm not of the age to become addicted to the feed. I close the thought and put it away. The period contains the thought. The lack makes it impossible to step away.

25 September, Kaohsiung

The US presidential election of 2020 is over. People are literally dancing in the streets. It's a reactive joy, a joy of negation, the kind of joy that looks like a people liberated from occupation. The city is in rubble, the Biden/Harris tanks have rolled in, and soon comes the reckoning. Did we bring this on ourselves? How did we get to that point? I don't think it will be that kind of reckoning though. There's no actual rubble to pick up, because the bombing campaign of the last four years consisted primarily of tweets, re-tweets and news reports about tweets. This is the war of our time. Harmful, toxic, psychologically violent, but like so much of our lived experience now, there were no events, no memories. It all took place over our screens, from the safe distance of being offended. It was the kind of tyranny we voluntarily consumed, nothing so material that we can't forget it. He was our *jouissance*, our delightful object of hatred. We laughed, we reproduced, we mimicked, we shared. We liked it.

What do we do now, when we've lost this precious object that fuels our reactive desires? At some point in Biden's 2021, we'll realize that we haven't solved anything. We'll continue the day to day, as billionaires find new and innovative ways to profit off of our compliance and suffering as we live in isolation from one another. Newer technologies will keep us further separated and will be marketed as an exciting advancement in human potential. And we will never demand that these billionaires of genuine oppression pay us back for it. But we should. We should make a stand based on this inhuman structure of unfairness in the accumulation of wealth.

Neoliberalism experienced its youthful exuberance under Thatcher and Reagan, but its marriage with techno-capitalism was arranged by Clinton-Gore, managed through Bush, and thrived through Obama. American power is not dual, it's monist. It has One Substance, sold through two manufactured and self-nurturing machines: the conservative and the liberal. Voting means that every slave gets to argue for the legitimacy of his master. If our master is elected, we leave with the feeling of having won—we won the game and the other side lost.

A common tactic of Democratic Party voters in this game is to chastise and shame the other team for voting against their interests. Republican politicians use guns and God to coerce their voters to vote for regressive taxation policies and old school corporate power, which conspires to keep them in economic poverty. Democratic politicians have their own coercion. They pitch technology, software and automation as a panacea. Well trained in Silicon Valley venture capitalist messaging and marketing, they pitch policies that maintain a techno-capitalist power structure—a new liberal wealth-generating machine to stand alongside the older conservative one. The two together strengthen the One Substance.

In this newer liberal power structure, we're more than consumers, we're "users." Everyone gets to operate the tools of self-expression that increase the power of the One Substance. Through our use, identities are built (and used), facts are accumulated (and used), sides are ossified (becoming both hard and brittle). Far more pernicious than the marketing of products toward a receptive demographic by psychological methods, individual psychologies are now constructed for active technological participation. This is the difference today. Things don't happen to us. Through use, we do the things that produce the grooves of anxiety-inducing self-habituation. This machine is fueled by narcissism, conformity and identity, a gathering snowball of awful that runs in perfect harmony with Trumpism. Our digital self-expressions are tracked and accumulated as data—a machine-learning for the production of new forms of self-exploitation.

This is the garden of liberal wealth. It allures through a different kind of desire. It profits from voluntary self-structuring as we find ourselves scattered and confused, swept along the acceleration of information. People too often misunderstand how power functions. Power, emboldened by the wealth we feed to it through our use, is neither an entity nor a person. It is an assemblage, a collective God we make, one that moves at the speed of participation and accumulates opportunities based on such habits.

Donald Trump isn't the cause of our horror, he's the effect of the architecture we used, contributed to, identified with, and voted for. That's the twisted irony in this epic tragedy. He may be a narcissist. But he's also the most natural outcome of the narcissism we all continue to express. We, the good team, planted the seeds of Trumpism that led to Trump.

In light of this reality, it doesn't surprise me that to so many, guns and God feel far more materially real (in the Jamesean sense of "real belief") than all this atheist digital irreality, performative sincerity, and false connectivity. Perhaps this is a major factor in why the vote was so razor-thin, why it wasn't an outright slaughter. Republicans haven't yet left the place of matter and spirit. They haven't forgotten these aspects of life that are present, immediate and local, which are integral to family and home. There is fear and hate. But this other world is pretty scary, this digital lifeworld, a world of appearances posing as activism for self-aggrandizement. We manifest Apollo's masks while denying Dionysus' soul. We have scattered our presents/presence into terrifying futures. Whichever POTUS holds office is neither the problem nor the solution to any of this. The problems are structural and psychological—the assemblages we accept and the narcissism we produce.

I suspect that this new generation of progressives doesn't really have an interest in change. They've become the puritanical alliance party, the party of correct, the supreme virtue, the good in forever wars over evil. They type in allegiances—with us or against us. Republicans used to talk in such language. All America has gone conservative and become fixed into righteous beliefs. We are too willing to manufacture and accumulate a side and use that gathered certainty to blame the other manufactured and accumulated side. With the allegiance manufactured and accumulated, we can then manufacture the other side, each of which consists of people we don't know and who as human beings always defy whatever is manufactured by the other.

This is why I, as a progressive, feel so out of place. Democrats have left me. But it's not just Democrats. All communication feels reactionary. All political discussion contributes to the hatred that responds to it. It is resentment versus resentment, Nietzsche's nightmare scenario.

What to do? By all signs, Bidenism seems to merely be anti-Trumpist, which means the world is still Trumpist. To overcome this, to be progressive, we need to stop reacting and turn toward what is active. Active doesn't mean to do more things, it means to arrange forces in a way that accumulates into new thought and new ideas. We need to figure out a way to slow down, stop growing, to reconsider how we consume, what we use, how we live, how we think, what we accept, and what we choose to participate in. We need to address the way power accumulates and stop legitimizing the harmful mechanisms we grant power to through our use.

To me, there are three pressing issues facing our future, all actionable and all involving the whole of society, indeed the whole of the planet: 1) economic inequality, 2) AI and technological acceleration, 3) global ecology. I am an ally of radical re-valuations of these three actionable areas. Grievances are legitimate. It is genuinely sad how ruthless and unfair history has been. There should be a path toward addressing the wrongs of history. But this cannot be the extent of it, this mass psychotherapy. Progressivism needs to progress, to become active rather than reactive. These three aspects—the value of work, the value of knowledge, and the health of the planet—all open to active forms of participation. They are not what divides, separates or categorizes. They are what we all share, regardless of party.

27 September, Kaohsiung

> "'The strong always have to be defended against the weak.'"
>
> - Friedrich Nietzsche[31]

Reading sections 8 and 9 from Chapter 2 of Deleuze's *Nietzsche and Philosophy*. I'm seeing such a statement in an entirely new way through Deleuze. Quotes such as these get Nietzsche into trouble, and give me pause, but through Deleuze's "Origin and Inverted Image" section—and indeed the whole book leading up to this point—we find that power constitutes a reversal. An image of the reversal forms in which dialectics and utility produces a subtraction of active, affirmational forces.

The strong and the weak then are not people. They are forces. The weak are reactive, opportunistic; they decompose and separate the strong so that the strong becomes subsumed by the weak. This is Nietzsche's "reactive triumph," the resentment and bad conscience that separates the strength of affirmation from its ability to accumulate.

We have to start thinking of politics in terms of *forces* as will-to-power.

5 October, Kaohsiung

As the news of the president's Covid-positive health situation streams forth, a mediated symphony develops in perfect harmony:

---

[31] *The Will to Power* (1968, Vintage Books).

1. The dominant melody: the president's undulating health status.

2. The lower third: the rising and falling of the stock market in pitch-perfect accordance with his undulating health status.

3. The higher fifth: the for-profit, corporate-owned news media and its steady stream of updates on the synchrony of the rising and falling of the stock market in pitch-perfect accordance with his undulating health status.

A three-part harmony of the cosmos, singing the song of modern-day power.

6 October, Kaohsiung

I think the reason I enjoy reading the ancient religious texts so much is that their authors are so deeply in love.

25 October, Kaohsiung

Facts make it easier to avoid thinking about incalculable things. Or, in a variation by Adam Staley Groves: "Numbers make it easier to avoid thinking about immeasurable things."[32]

Both statements reveal a similar problem in this new alliance between liberalism and institutionalism: the need to verify so that we may judge and, as usually results, dismiss. We do this so that we may forget, or as we say, "move on." (We vote for the same reason, to

---

[32] This comes from a Facebook post he wrote around this time.

forget.) We do this in the midst of accelerated lived experience, failing as we do to account for the externalities and resonances of such experience that surrounded the fact, the number.

If you are my friend, a true friend—by that I mean if I love you—I will defend you to the end. This would make me a horrible billionaire, or politician, or celebrity. I'm grateful to have the privilege of being none of those things. But hopefully it means that I can be there to love you in the face of judgment and dismissal. I will always choose the intimate over the universal. One is felt, the other determined.

"Zoom rhymes with tomb." (A.S.G.)

*****

Not everyone thinks in the same way. Until now, that truth has been invisible. When we see someone walking down the street, we don't know what that person thinks. But now we can know it, we see it visibly in the political expression that is the mask: some people think differently from other people. Not everyone has faith in science, they have faith in other things.

I'm at a loss to understand the rabid resistance by the non-maskers. It's something we marvel at over here in Asia. But I do suspect that there are a lot of people who just don't care about other people, and don't care about the public good. Masking is not only conformity, it's a confirmation that liberalism is the higher virtue, that the system works for all. Non-masking is an expression of their inner Bruce Willis, all the film heroes we've internalized. It's the dark underbelly of every motivational speaker who has said "find your own path." Thus turned, it's like Christopher Nolan's *The Dark Knight*: "Some people just want to watch the world burn." When you feel the world has done you wrong—and it's true in so many ways—why give a rat's ass about the public good?

If we had the courage and the conduit to deal with the problem of economic inequality, if there were any political party that championed this, so many of these antagonisms and flashpoints we have now (racial, biological, misogynistic othering) would lose their reactive power. And I know this because I've lived in countries over here in Asia that take care of their citizens' basic needs, rather than this bootstraps bullshit that both parties propagate, and which American culture fosters.

If we concentrated on common needs we wouldn't need to fight each other. But I suspect the anti-maskers, at a deep level, feel left out of a civilization fixated on politically correct discourse. They have been abandoned in today's two-party system of neoliberal centrism on the one hand and wealth-hoarding on the other. Left out of the party, some turn to darker thoughts, with Trump as their champion, the only one who speaks them. At this level, I kinda get it. Fuck social decency, what has society ever done for me? Let it burn.

5 November, Kaohsiung

Still reading Deleuze reading Nietzsche...

Jesus was the son of Paul. If he were the son of God, he'd be Buddha.

7 November, Kaohsiung

There's this bizarre video making the rounds of Trump protesters rocking out to Rage Against the Machine. And at first you might think, well that's weirdly ironic, what machine are they raging against? Because Trump is the capitalist machine.

I suspect that the machine they're raging against is not this, but the other one, the Democratic Party machine. And while I doubt there's much thought behind this rage, it is... rage. Rage isn't rational, it's reactive. There are so many DNC machines, real and imagined: there's the socialist machine (which doesn't actually exist, but is made scary through intentionally bad interpretations), there's the cultural machine of liberal media (MSNBC, BLM, rainbow flags, and other assorted fears that liberals are pushing upon them), and there's the techno-capitalist/neoliberal machine (the very real one that has automated their jobs away and kept them closed out of the new economy and new language that liberals currently enjoy).

I wish we could get past the manufactured dualisms that have ossified in our animal brains, and see the light of the One Substance of American power that abuses us all. They are crafty puppeteers who produce two different illusions. These illusions are what people vote for: culture/progress/Science/normal or tradition/ liberty/God/normal. The outcome of this illusionary participation is a victory of degrees, not of kind: the Centrist power or the Conservative power.

The rages, meanwhile, are caught up raging over the illusions: The socialist rage is a myth that even dems believe but only because they believe the other believes it, so they also vote against their illusion about the illusion. But the corporate and techno-capitalist rage is very real. It manifests in two forms: the Centrist-

Democrat and Conservative-Republican machines of power and wealth. They appear different because they message things in clever subtleties of phrase that appeal to each prisoner. But they are both about maintaining the mastery of wealth and power.

I can't help but wonder... if we stopped fighting over the illusory rage, we might actually be able to confront the real rage, and in making headway there, we might even be able to make some progress on the cultural rage and make strides toward equality... not to mention the immediate crisis of ecology and the whole host of other global disasters we're ignoring right now.

This is another way of saying what is perhaps a tired old idea: that if we stopped fighting amongst ourselves we might actually be able to handle the core problems of wealth, power and technology. This is the factory, the machine, that produces the resentment of the other.

13 November, Kaohsiung

Philosophy lies in between science and fiction.

Or in post-Hellenistic terms, between *logos* and *mythos*.

14 November, Kaohsiung

There is a saying, common among self-professed rationalists: "facts don't care about your feelings." This statement ignores the deeper truth: "feelings don't care about your facts."

I don't want to live in a world of facts. I don't care, in a world of facts. I want to live in a world of sensation.

Machines care about facts; people need to care more about feelings.

15 November, Kaohsiung

Pluralism is not the same thing as relativism. The latter is associated with being, the former with becoming. Or if that's too abstract: To argue for relativism is to argue that truth is based on how one approaches the object of study; to argue for pluralism is to argue that anything we name as this object has multiple things going on depending on how it is arranged or how it arranges itself. Relativism is a claim about how we study something. Pluralism does not care about your study. It is already underway, has already taken action, and as it affects you it is doing so at the level of sensation. To take advantage of what is plural requires attention, an attitude not of seeing but of listening.

Pluralism is not in opposition to monism: any *thing* is both one and many. If pluralism is against anything it is dialectical reasoning. A dialectical method pits two opposing ideas against each other. The dialectic has negation and contradiction built in. The classic idea comes in Plato's dialogues, but perhaps the most famous example is the master/slave dialectic. As Deleuze writes about Nietzsche, only the slave thinks in dialectics. And this is why we maintain the hierarchy that we deserve. The master produces morality; the slave adopts the idea and employs it in dialectical forms, through negation, contradiction and opposition. The slave is fueled in dialectical reasoning by a host of afflictions: resentment, bad conscience, suffering and guilt. Such afflictions are then projected onto perceived others. This not only applies to Christians; atheists are stuck in the same trap, except that they have replaced God with Reason and Knowledge.

What Deleuze is drawing out of Nietzsche is the problem of reactionary morality at the cost of affirmation. The dialectic at its most binary is entirely reactive. It pits one manufactured side against another, while those who hold the machinery of power benefit from this struggle. It's been going on this way for centuries. In 1990, there was hope that digital information technologies would solve this problem—a pluralistic technology to break apart hard power. But as Deleuze and Nietzsche (and so many other philosophers) warned us, power is an assemblage that gathers, adapts and finds new means of control. The internet failed once it got swept up in the production of capital. What promised plurality 30 years ago ended up congealing into two equally divided streams of Knowledge. Dialectics *as a practice* is reinforced by it, and is now stronger than anything history could have imagined.

In 2020, we live in a world of pluralism, but we talk and think as though the world were dialectical. This is why our politics and our discourse appears so cleanly divided into two equal sides. We've become awash in appearances manufactured by media channels to think A versus B. It is the most simplistic and functional way to think, a clean manufacturing of two valid opposites.

The dialectic produces a reaction. This is why all of our political engagement is only reactive. Biden was not an affirmation; he is a reaction to Trump. Trumpism is reactive to liberal moral judgment. Etcetera. It's all one big cycle of resentment and reaction. (Bernie Sanders was instead the affirmation, but the DNC couldn't let that happen because they gain by maintaining the dialectic).

The way to break this is by thinking in a plural manner, of a third, fourth and fifth way. And to do this, we have to first recognize that A versus B only maintains the one power that preserves itself while it oppresses everyone. For Nietzsche and Deleuze, we have to understand power in a different way; it is not a thing to defeat, nor a division between, but rather an arrangement of forces. Power is an assemblage that moves, develops and forms into something. It takes advantage of a populace who have divided themselves by the knowledge that is consumed.

Life, lived experience, the sensation that Nietzsche and Deleuze emphasize so strongly, is plural. Life produces difference. Deleuze is known as the philosopher of difference, and he finds an ally in Nietzsche's pluralism. Difference is non-dialectical. Difference does not play the game of this versus that, instead it moves along what is plural, what is other than the dialectical exchange. Difference is an active force, generative, an affirmation of the will.

> "Nietzsche's 'yes' is opposed to the dialectical 'no'; affirmation to dialectical negation; difference to dialectical contradiction; joy, enjoyment, to dialectical labour; lightness, dance, to dialectical responsibilities."33

Difference as an ethics, as a politics, arranges thought as a topology rather than a line. Will-to-power is the affirmation of difference.

The scary thing to me about the future of Trumpism, which seems potent enough to survive long into the future, is how it is able to embrace plurality far better than Democrats can, but only in a reactive sense and one that constructs oppositions from it. Someone more intellectually capable than Trump will come along and assemble all of this resentment and bad faith in far more clever ways into something even more horrific and adaptable. Reactive forces arrange a battleground that favors hatred because it is constantly producing

---

33 Gilles Deleuze, *Nietzsche and Philosophy* (1983, Columbia University Press).

otherness. That's why the "Socialist" tag works—it is reactionary and divisive *between Democrats*. Old guard Democrats fear the reaction, so they themselves react rather than offer something to affirm. New guard Democrats are playing their own reactive game—pitting us against each other, testing purity, casting blame, determining allies, excluding fringe thought. Identity is a series of divisive reactions. Identity and negation lie at the core of dialectical strategies. Affirmation is a recognition of the power of differences.

My hope is that something affirmational emerges from the plurality that is materially real but now lies fallow. It requires difference to open a new thought, a "line of flight" as Deleuze so often says. That's hard to do in this dialectical knowledge that we fight so hard to maintain.

28 November, Kaohsiung

Why do "they" dismiss scientific facts? Perhaps because they intuit that facts privilege the fact-producers more than those who toil in the immediate actuality of machinery and labor.

*****

There is a grocery store in Denmark that demands, via an emoji clue from a monitor, that one can only enter if one first smiles. Reading about this pulled me straight to Byung-Chul Han's "burnout society" concept and the clinical problem of excessive positivity, which is a common strategy of control in 2020.

"The society of positivity, from which negativity has disappeared, is a society of bare life, which is dominated exclusively by the concern 'to make sure of survival' in the face of discontinuity. This is a slave's life." [34]

"Like hysteria or mourning, melancholy is a phenomenon of negativity, whereas depression involves excess positivity." The "violence of positivity... expresses itself as the exhaustion and inclusion that characterize the society of achievement. ... Today violence issues more readily from the conformism of consensus than from the antagonism of dissent." [35]

Han's critique, responding primarily to Nietzsche, is not about the positive or negative *individual*, but the very *conditions* of positivity at the societal level. His contention is that we live in a time that is "poor in negativity," meaning that negativity is cast aside. Society deals instead with a kind of quantitative positivity—an excess or a deficiency. For Han, today's means of societal control is to amplify positivity, producing an excess. Because negativity has been stripped away—we maybe can say "shamed"—value functions as degrees of positivity. This for Han is a clinical problem, leading to the demand to cure oneself of any negativity.

This demand—the pressure of achieving and being continually confronted with such pressure—produces fertile ground for depression. It's not that the individual has an excess of positivity, but that excessive positivity produces a kind of condition that is viral —a demand that one conform to the pressures of positive consensus. On some level, we know this but lack a means of action (resonating Nietzsche here). This is why Han is critical of Hannah Arendt's *vita*

---

[34] Byung-Chul Han, *The Agony of Eros* (2017, MIT Press).

[35] Han, *The Burnout Society* (2015, Stanford University Press).

activa, or active life. It exacerbates the problem, producing increased conditions that may lead to depression.

I find a lot of examples of this pressure to be positive, to achieve, to smile, and it seems the world keeps getting sadder, not happier. I see this viral condition strongly permeating places I've lived in Asia, such as Korea, China and Taiwan. I suspect it's because, like this video, machines are producing the images of happiness that are a mask of conformity and control. As Han writes, it's much easier to produce a violence of positivity than a violence of negativity.

"The violence of positivity does not deprive, it saturates; it does not exclude, it exhausts. That is why it proves inaccessible to unmediated perception. ... Depression, ADHD, and burnout syndrome point to excess positivity. Burnout syndrome occurs when the ego overheats, which follows from too much of the Same."[36]

Any psychological condition is extraordinarily complex, and cannot be reduced to societal conditions, just as it cannot be attributed solely to individual actions. And this is the key point. We think of something like positivity as an entirely existential issue, that it lies entirely with the individual. Han is pointing to a systemic problem, one *manifest* in individuals. I see so much of this in 2020. It is expressed in narcissistic social media sharing tendencies, but also in determinations of the societal *value* of mobile technology in business practices, higher education, and, it seems... grocery stores. Positivity is a condition in which the human psyche is tightly bound with technology. This becomes a problem when it is employed as an unconscious means of conformity, control and consensus.

---

[36] Ibid.

2 December, Kaohsiung

I'm working on an essay on the ancient concept of *logos* by reading a history of first century Christianity, while also engaged in an almost year-long project now of reading Nietzsche. It's in simultaneous readings like these where philosophy becomes so interesting.

Philo is an interesting fulcrum for early Christianity. For him, *logos* lies *between* Goodness (Creative Power) and Authority (Regent Power, governing). The first is God, the second is Lord. The Creative came first, the Regent second (even though they are, in God, essentially timeless), because Authority and Lord presided over what is already made.

If we consider the influence Christianity has on our embedded cultural unconscious, our "feel" for the mechanism of power has an element of substance/being/essence as preceding authority/law/manifestation. Between the two is the utterance/action of the Word (Christian *logos*) that defines essence as a means of governance. Goodness is essential, already made, power as substance. Authority is made through the power of the expression, the utterance, the act of governing. Goodness is God; Authority is Lord. Between the two is *Logos* with a capital L.

This is quite a stranglehold. Even in liberal atheism today, the power of Authority always has Essence as a constant. No matter what we do as citizens, we feel at a deep level that essence dominates. Further, this essence is Good, which is not only impenetrable but conceptually unassailable. Capitalism functions this way, as the Goodness behind all our labor and work, offering us the idea of earthly salvation.

Moving to Nietzsche then, his bold move is taking on not only Authority as power, but Goodness as power—Good and Evil, two aspects of power that function as a collective psychology, as unconscious thought dwelling in the minds and the mind of Europe (and by extension today, America, and by further extension, the post-Globalist world as a whole, at least in economic practices). It's not enough to attack the agents, the Regent Power, the governors, the Lord aspect of divine law; Goodness itself must be scrutinized as the essence from which power is manifest through behavior.

6 **December, Kaohsiung**

Deleuze is Wittgenstein in reverse, at least as pertaining to the possibilities of thought, action and expression.

23 **December, Kaohsiung**

For all this studying, reading and writing I've been working on this year—Nietzsche, the Hellenistic era, early Christianity; the transition from Greek questions, to Christian answers, to Roman law; I've come to the following conclusions:

1. Nature is immanent

2. Thought transcends

3. Power assembles

4. All "western" consciousness, even atheism, is Christian.

26 December, Kaohsiung

They'll call it the year of the pandemic. But it should be called the year of *I can't breathe*. The coronavirus is just one manifestation of a viral time, when digital asphyxiation finally became biological.

I can't breathe is George Floyd. He named the year. His expression triggered a viral (and needed) mobilization of Black Lives Matter. It ran headlong into the virality of white anger and hatred, which turns to opposition and violence, and from this mutated uneasily into another virality of white guilt, which unwittingly commandeers a black movement for its own psyche.

I can't breathe is an ecological condition.[37] Despite my hopes, the pandemic did nothing to heal the planet of its viral pollutants. Airplane emissions went down, but that did not offset other pollutants. People stayed inside and consumed energy, ordered packages, bought new screens, and sent UberEats vehicles zipping around neighborhoods (increasing the wealth of some of the shadiest businessmen we have today). Rather than go outside, people burned air conditioning units and centralized home heating systems.

I can't breathe is a Californian choking on forest fires made viral by a planet that is too hot and too consumptive to correct itself by its own means. Because the Democratic Party is caught up in the same techno-capitalist and neoliberal agenda as Republicans, there's no party with enough power to stop the conflagration from spreading further.

I can't breathe has been mutating in Asia since the onslaught of globalization, and increases every year. China's pollutants eased for a little while, resulting in crystal clear blue skies across the straight

---

[37] See https://www.theverge.com/22178714/2020-nature-heal-pollution-greenhouse-gases-emissions-dip-covid.

here in Taiwan. But China's economic exhale is now back to choke-inducing levels. Air pollution is something North Americans and Western Europeans ignore, since it only affects those *others*—South Americans, Asians, Africans. Air pollution now kills an estimated 8.8 million people per year (one out of every eight people on the planet).[38] Covid killed 1.7 million people this year.[39] When I first started going to Chiang Mai in 2012, the polluted season ran from early March to end of April. Now it's half the year, beginning in November and lingering through May. Air pollution is the virality of consumption. More cars, more industry, more toys, more exotic farms to satisfy "new money" demand in China and other parts of the world. The increasing inequality of wealthy-to-poor is fueling so much of this. Poor people burning coal to stay warm, wealthy people burning fuel and forests for its consumers.

I can't breathe is a Hong Kong protester choking on teargas while fighting for a future. This was the hopeful virus of the past two years, a shining example of how to mutate and spread, to bend, to flow. This new China economy was the origin of so much harmful virology and *virality*—biological, chemical, consumptive, ideological. But Chinese thinking, in a far older, pre-capitalist sense, offers a way through. The fluidity of Chinese thought opens other strategies that move around and through what is not immediately evident. Hong Kong did it so impressively until Beijing finally channelled some old school power, laying down the hammer of State control.

I can't breathe is a person dying on a ventilator, or struggling at home, coughing up an illness that originated from the consumption of meat and which was spread by the ubiquity of cheap, fuel-consumptive travel. Why did Taiwan win in keeping Covid out when

---

[38] See https://academic.oup.com/cardiovascres/article/116/11/1910/5770885.

[39] Retrieved Dec. 26 from https://www.worldometers.info/coronavirus/. Note that these numbers can be disputed due to pre-existing conditions, as to whether there is a direct causality between diagnosis and death.

the USA and others couldn't? One reason never discussed is that the USA is afraid of offending China for economic reasons. Taiwan, meanwhile, was the only nation in the world with the independence to flip a middle finger at China. They shut down incoming flights from the mainland immediately because they don't care what the mainland thinks. The USA-China connection is a virus of globalization, wealth and economic opportunity. America, and every other competitive nation on Earth, is owned by the Chinese market.

I can't breathe is a plea to wear masks so we can breathe again. But Americans aren't good at viral thinking, not yet. They're trained for pragmatics, oppositions, objects to identify and eliminate, something to shoot at. I can't get angry at a person for not wanting to wear a mask. Americans live through faces. They haven't been conditioned for invisibles and they thrive on their independence from mandates imposed by others. This is its own virus—a mutating lack of image-free imagination.

I can't breathe because the world is viral. It is composed of all these overlapping and intersecting viruses of thought, matter, biology and power. And it will continue as long as our consumptions continue, as long as the desire for normal continues. Virality is driven by an unconscious desire to spread into bodies, systems, structures and minds. Consumption fuels its spread. Consumption drives thought such as "get the economy going again" without considering that this overwhelmingly benefits the wealthy. They can breathe. The rest of us are content being evangelists for our chosen master: Science or God. We fail to see the overlaps, the movements, the interrelations. In life after God, Americans have forgotten how to look up, to see who owns them. We still have not figured out that ignorance doesn't reside so much in your neighbor, but is instead deep inside our shared culture. The virus of ignorance surges the more we choose not to change. Like a sneeze in a crowded elevator that remains hovering in the air, waiting for new bodies.

31 December, Kaohsiung

I'm reading Han's concept of the swarm and his idea of "addition." I've been proposing an ethics of "and," which Han would criticize. I understand his argument. "And" and "addition" multiplies noise; nothing lingers. In a world of "and" we have too much information. But the problem he avoids is the other issue—the problem of "one." In the midst of this "and," a digital consumer reduces to "one" in order to make sense of the seeming disorder. This is how digitally induced knowledge streams form. The "one" idea, thought, "being," etc. that one selects is easily adaptable to one's own sense of conviction. In "one," one conviction, one path, is fostered and nurtured. It's as if each person has his or her own personal god.

We are at this in-between point where we are acclimated to states of nature and laws within that nature. We remain creatures of discipline. Digital is *another* nature that overlaps the organic and we interact with it through the same expressions of memory, belief, understanding and communicating. We are not digital enough to handle this conversion because *this particular* form of "and" is manufactured and inorganic. Yet we engage as if we were dealing with the chaos of nature.

Without one God to turn to, each of us invents our own One that conforms to our habits and belief structures. We seek out others who go to the same church, feel the same knowledge stream, and cannot see the other ones that pile up. They are just noise.

Han is right about the problems of "and," but the other problem is that of "one"—the one *shaped from the and*, not the *and itself*. If we could, each of us, express more Spinozan joy within the streams from the and, we'd be healthier thinkers and believers. It remains a matter of what we wish to linger *in*.

FRAGMENTS 6: 2021

1 January, Kaohsiung

I'm starting the new year as I like in this year of isolation, by sitting in a cafe and reading, this time Han's *In the Swarm*. My thoughts dwell on natality, action and leisure in this birth of a new year, of overcoming the "bare life" mentality of 2020 and its rational ethics of confinement, achievement, sacrifice and exploitation.

> "Action means performing a deed that inaugurates something unprecedented, something wholly other. Natality, being born, provides its ontological condition. Every birth promises a radical beginning. Likewise, acting means making a new start, opening up another world. ... Is action, in the strong sense, still possible today? Isn't everything we do so fully at the mercy of automatic processes that even the miracle of a radical new beginning can no longer break their hold? Are we still subjects making decisions for ourselves? Haven't the digital and capitalist machines formed an uncanny alliance that annihilates all freedom of action? Aren't we living, today, in a *time of the undead*, when not just *being born* but even *dying* has been rendered impossible? ... *Bare life*—that is, life that is to be prolonged at any cost—knows neither birth nor death. The time of the digital is a *postnatal* and *postmortal* era." [40]

---

[40] All quotes in this entry: Byung-Chul Han, *In the Swarm* (2017, MIT Press).

Today we are always working. Today's techno-capitalism is the era of the eternal worker. Even leisure time is in service to productivity—the impossibility of a true withdrawal, the inability to leave, the endless streams of always-available. To overcome this, we need to activate new fields of play and leisure—not to slow down time against acceleration, rather to open "a separate time," one that staves off the present "dystopia of achievement and exploitation."

In other words, we need not leisure as a temporary break in service to productivity, but leisure as an act of opening "another kind of temporality."

3 January, Kaohsiung

Nietzsche's eternal recurrence: A time-based response to Kant. Not an as-if directed as universal law contained within finite time, rather an as-if with a recognition of time's infinite possibility.

4 January, Kaohsiung

A definition of *tyranny* by John Locke, which I came across as Trump and the forces of resentment are aiming to delegitimize and divide:

> "He *acts* also *contrary to his trust*, when he either employs the force, treasure, and offices of the society, to corrupt the *representatives*, and gain them to his purposes; or openly pre-engages the *electors*, and prescribes to their choice, such, whom he has, by solicitations, threats, promises, or otherwise, won to his designs; and employs

them to bring in such, who have promised before-hand what to vote, and what to enact."[41]

9 January, Seoul

Call this "A Monist Perspective On the United States of America"...

I've developed a little rule in my 14 years living outside of my country of birth: If you're not a US citizen, I'll listen to your impressions and your criticisms of my home country, but not your judgments. It's like that great takeaway line from *The Last Black Man in San Francisco*—"You don't get to hate it unless you love it." Hate and love only come through having lived the joy and the hardship.

I don't presume to "know" Taiwan, or England, or anywhere else. I can't essentialize it, only observe my movement through it. I would hope others feel the same, but America as the object is often placed at a different level. Recent political events have magnified this difference, leading to a change in attitude. People used to ask me questions. They still do, but with less tolerance in awaiting a response; now it has shifted to judgment and facts delivered *to me*. You may have gathered some facts, but you don't get to judge if you've never lived it.

Perhaps a little Spinozan monism will help.

Life manifests in attributes, taking on some mode of expression. The attribute is not essence but constitutes it. In other

---

[41] John Locke, *Second Treatise on Government* (1980, Hackett Publishing), Ch. XIX, "Of the Dissolution of Government." After listening to an episode of *The Partially Examined Life* podcast posted on Dec. 21, 2020, available here, https:// partiallyexaminedlife.com/2020/12/21/reissue-ep37-locke-politics/, I transcribed here the quote mentioned on the show from the original text from the Hackett publication.

words, whatever happens—whatever is expressed in thought or matter—is *of* essence but also is what *makes* essence. The whole, the substance, God if you wish to think that way, expresses through the attribute. Think of an impossibly complex octopus but with infinite tentacles—a *multipus*. One of its tentacles touches something prickly and the multipus recoils. The tentacle wasn't randomly doing something; the multipus made it happen. But in so doing, the multipus changes, while also retaining its essence. Now, think of life as an infinite array of tentacles. Each one expresses in a way that is both independent and inseparable from essence.

The pandemic is revealing that the world is made up of many essences, many *multipi*.[42] To me, it *seems as though* (my impression) Taiwan is a multipus whose tentacles have wrapped around itself. The USA is a multipus flailing about as it always does. Taiwan keeps its tentacles pretty close anyway, gingerly poking here and there. So closing in is not antithetical to its essence. The USA is not changing at all. But it is adapting.

The point of this metaphor is that the States seems out of its mind right now. But one thing its citizens do, what *we* do, is flail our tentacles. We test, push and experiment. We are restless, and this emerges at times in fearful and reactionary ways and other times in fearless and experimental ways. It's all *essentially* American. We don't change our substance, but we do adapt, and in doing so, essence *modifies*. The USA right now is testing itself, pushing itself, expressing itself. Existing understandings are being challenged, the structures that hold it together are being shaken. This is what pliable societies do. It's the ones who do not move that suffer a hard crash.

---

[42] I'm taking liberties with Spinoza's philosophy because for him there can be only one *multipus*, not many. What I describe as a multipus is rather *itself* a mode. But I'm applying the concept of substance to the idea of scale without infinite regress. In my metaphor, the one substance-multipus is the planet, while each nation is its own multipus. This wouldn't be a mode, but its own entity whose expressions come through modes of expressing.

Any American who says "Just stay home" is, in terms of essence, an anomaly. It's an expression that is out of line with the essence of its multipus. One may be *correct* in saying *stay at home*—in a wider, global *one substance*—but *stay at home* is not a normal American "expression." Stay at home is expressing panic, and thus looking to *other multipi* for something different, another substance to borrow from. It's one that wants to give in to State control to manage the appearance of chaos, some other, more exotic octopus that holds tightly to the body. Stay at home is the expression that throws up its hands and says "We're moving to Canada!" Except in this case, it says "Why can't we be more like China?"

This brings me to the civil unrest over the past 10 months. What I see in our socially mediated discourse is a battle over modes. For Spinoza, everything is an expression of God. This is what makes him such a beautiful thinker. All is immanent, all is expression. You are a mode of God; every time you brush your teeth you are expressing God's essence. (Spinoza names God "Substance," and if one wishes, one can use that term as well; philosophers call this "monism.") You are a *mode*. Your body is a mode. Your thought comes through a mode, expressing an attribute of substance and thus expressing its essence. A mode, as I'm reading Spinoza, is a *form* of the attribute, a vehicle through which something is expressed. A mode is an actual thing whose activity expresses essence. A mode is an "affection" (expression of essence) of the attributes of substance. A thought comes through a mode of thinking. So does an act of the will.

We've been seeing each other as different substances expressing different essences. This is how *othering* happens—seeing the other as divided from oneself. Ideas such as good or evil, reality and perfection, are modes of thinking that happen through separation, and we are seeing a new era of separation that leads down dangerous pathways of thought and action. But we could otherwise conceive of a body, a person, as a mode through which an idea is expressed. As Deleuze puts it, these differences are not of divisions of substance, they are a "modifications" (mode-ification) of substance.[43] Again, each mode expresses substance which in turn changes substance.

We think that thought and action, good and evil, etc. are directed outside of us somehow, transcendent to us like a God, unapproachable and unassailable. Atheists have internalized this tradition, but they supplant Law or Custom for God. Writing about Spinoza, Deleuze suggests that his famous book *Ethics* is "a typology of immanent modes of existence." As modal, an immanent "ethics" replaces a transcendent Morality with a capital M. In Spinoza, nothing is separate, there is no division of substance, there is only a mode of expression.

So, I'm thinking of America in this Spinozan sense of expression and its modes—the one multipus and its many tentacled attributes that express in modes. To put this more plainly, Taiwan's multipus closes in on itself; in times of stress, it wraps its tentacles even more tightly around its body and preserves itself. The US multipus flails; it reaches out and grabs, tests, tastes, touches, explores, and very often finds its expression stuck in a power outlet, shocking the entire substance. But it is also creative, experimental, and figures shit out sometimes.

This does not mean that people are not accountable for their actions. We are. Behavior and psychology are immeasurable, and to some incalculable degree everyone has a choice to be stupid, to give into hate, to lack a sense of patience and empathy, to ignore the lives and livelihoods of others, to reduce a person to a category. These are choices. But they're also born of conditions of experimentation.

These modes and attributes of the US multipus run into trouble when one mode has decided it is *the mode*. This is how

---

[43] All quotes here are from Gilles Deleuze, *Spinoza: Practical Philosophy* (1988, City Lights Books).

intolerant attributes/expressions that have accumulated great wealth, power and influence have historically harmed the whole multipus. Over the past generation, atheists, recognizing the emergence of science as a dominant mode of power, have adopted many of the same modes of expression. Here are some of the different ways in which the US multipus runs into trouble:

Law and Punishment. The United States of America has always been a nation predicated on punishment rather than encouragement. Our historical Christian divine Law lives on through an atheist transcendental law that is adjudicated everywhere by everybody: the finger wagging discouragement of wrongdoing. Many people know that the Democrat politician functions by enacting new laws that make little sense to others within the multipus who are not happy about them. This dissonance of "sense"—as in, "this doesn't make sense to me"—festers through news and social media discourses.

Education and Work. The United States of America is a nation whose public and higher education systems are stripping away human-centered learning in ethics, humanities, philosophy, spirituality, critical thinking, traditional values, etc., and replacing them with ends-based techno-science, techno-capitalism, entrepreneurship, and other such commodity-based programming initiatives. These initiatives generate wealth for new liberal power but are soul-crushing to many in the multipus. As ends-based, education and work de-emphasize inquiry in the production of objects of practical knowledge. Those untrained in higher academia utilize *the very same* knowledge-product practices online, absorbing alternative "conspiracies" that the liberal elite ignores. So much of the "university" is now a training ground for careers in technologies of dehumanization. It functions to indoctrinate and empower the economically privileged for future economic advantage over others. In other words, liberalism is training young people for the new economy, whose products are used by *everyone*. It is the composition of a new nature. This produces a liberalist knowledge regime in which those *untrained* have no language for such nature, which results in reactive expressions—conspiracy, hate, etc. Many people in the multipus know on some level that this new wealth production scheme excludes them, and they are not happy about it.

The New Atheist Discourse. In addition to the massive shift to techno-capitalist economics and knowledge production, the USA is a nation whose liberal elite is also demanding that everyone conform to the new atheist law of puritanical morality. This means conforming to a language and discourse that makes little sense to so many in the multipus. A generation ago there were three words that were not allowed to be uttered; today you need a daily dictionary to keep up with what is permissible or impermissible. Every public statement has to be second-guessed for pitfalls of latent racism or misogyny; the expression needs to worm its way through one's intramental team of lawyers to gain approval before speaking. As expressed, its validity requires it to be correct or it will be corrected or shamed. A term like "cis" matters to someone who has a grasp of the liberal elite *nature*, who has training in or has enough friends trained in cultural studies academia; it's laughable to someone who does not. They know that this discourse excludes them, and they are not happy about it.

"Woke" is an interesting term for this. "Correctness" is juridicial, but "woke" is religious. It is Christian at its core. It presumes that someone "sees the light" in a religious sense, that one must awaken and come to hear ("obey") the righteous Word (*logos*) of the age. But "woke" is even more pernicious than a Christian awakening. In the Christian version, one comes to God personally, perhaps through an act of *encouragement*. Becoming woke, by contrast, *demands* that others join the church, having had no personal, divine experience. It is evangelical but at a more demanding and shaming level, that of *punishment*. Many people can't wake to this, and worse, few are taking the time to encourage them toward the atheist awakening. This is how everything in the multipus becomes reactionary, binary, confrontational and oppositional.

13 January, Seoul

Cults used to be places fragile and impoverished minds went to. One had to go out and cohabitate with others and share bodily in the self-delusion. Now—in this bio-viral age of lockdown, stay-at-home, and screen living, in this techno-viral age that encourages hypersubjectivity, narcissism and isolated anxiety—the cult comes to you. You don't have to go anywhere to begin your programming. The cult is the internet.

16 January, Seoul

An exercise in speculative fiction, with a happy ending...

2020: The world was hit with an epic pandemic that exposed every nation's degree of openness and control. We global citizens were stunned and remained in a state of shock throughout the year. In response, the US government exercised openness. Asian nations exercised various degrees of control. High levels of control led to greater containment.

2021: The change of year changed little. We learn that vaccines weren't the messiah that was promised and that this, all of this, is normal. 2020 set the ground for the efficacy of control/openness. In 2021, the triple yikes of domestic terror, civil unrest, and the ongoing pandemic will demand solutions. Presuming the insurrectional hate is dealt with at the level of law, it will retreat into the shadows come spring. But with Asian nations as the example, control will escalate, leading to a muted and mutated version of yikes. Because we couldn't control 2020, we will heed the rational argument for greater control in 2021. States of exception will multiply and we'll watch it happen, fenced in by our own personal screens.

2022: With a citizenry that willingly and necessarily gives itself over to control, 2022 becomes the year of resigned acceptance. The rationalists will retain control: fall in line, do the right thing, wear a mask, listen to authority, appeal to law, say all nice things or shut up. The screen-gazing Y Generation that dominates corporate media content production will fail to offer anything substantive, as they continue to be nurtured by the approval of criticism and litigating the behavior of presumed categories of people. They'll be right, morally, and that will suffice for the majority. Meanwhile, the backward, hate-mongering traditionalists will interact in the actual world of sensation. They'll get their hands dirty. Reactionary hate will adopt the techniques of progressive activism and we'll see pockets of this re-emerge within the structures of control. The screen-consuming, well-to-do masses will write about these pockets of resistance as they keep accepting control. It'll seem at times like the world is collapsing, but it will mostly be a year of *whatever* as consumption continues to uphold the economy and the society of control.

2023: It's just a feeling. No one knows how the various dominoes will stream along their various paths. But I do believe that the USA, at least, eventually gets out of this. Mistakes need to run their course, but Americans are, above all, creative problem solvers. Something will break in 2023. We will reach a point of turning away from control and self-imposed authority. We will realize that that we have been fighting amongst ourselves over identities that contain and divide us from each other. We'll decide that the management of permissible language was a bad idea. Perhaps the Zs will lead the way and find creative outlets to express difference within unity and take back sensory openness without violence. Artists will create again with a newfound sense of courage and we'll finally share an urgency about global ecology. I don't know how this will happen, but America usually finds a way. Resistance to control is a key element to seeing this world emerge, and resistance lies at the heart of US culture.

17 January, Seoul

When both the demons and the angels are rioting and destroying, maybe it's time to take a hard look at the church we've built.

27 January, Seoul

Reading Foucault's late lectures on care of the self...

After the arrival of Christianity came a continuance of life after death: eternal salvation. This also means that in life, one gave up responsibility of one's own death to God the sovereign. Before Christianity, one had to deal with death at a personal level. In life after God, today's atheist is once again with the ancients. One must face the crisis of one's own end.

For the Epicureans and the Stoics, old age was a gift, an achievement, indeed something to live one's life toward, rather than some impending existential, subconscious terror. For them, "old age constitutes the positive moment, the moment of fulfillment, the peak of this lengthy practice that the individual has pursued or had to submit to throughout his life. Freed from all physical desires and free from all the political ambitions he has renounced, with all the experience he has been able to acquire, the old man will be the person who is sovereign over himself and who can be entirely satisfied with himself. The old man has a definition in this history and in this form of the practice of the self: he is the one who can finally take pleasure in himself, be satisfied with himself, put all his joy and satisfaction in himself, without expecting pleasure, joy, or satisfaction from anything else, neither from physical pleasures, of which he is no longer capable, nor the pleasures of ambition, which he has given up. The old man then is someone who delights in himself, and the point at which old age arrives, if well-prepared by a long practice of the self, is the point at which, Seneca says, the self finally arrives at itself, at which one returns to one's self, and at which one has a perfect and complete relationship to the self of both mastery and satisfaction."[44]

Before them, the Pythagoreans noted four stages of life: you are a child for the first twenty years, an adolescent from twenty to forty, young from forty to sixty, and an old man after sixty. Perhaps picking up from this, Seneca wrote that sixty is old age, but isn't something we wait for. Rather, our post-sixty age is something we should prepare and practice for during our lifetime, "an old age we produce, as it were, which we practice." In pre-Christian existence, therefore, "we should place ourselves in a condition such that we live it as if it is already over." Old age is a positive goal: "We should strive towards old age and not resign ourselves to having it come upon us one day. Old age, with its own forms and values, should orientate the whole course of life."

---

[44] All quotes in this section are from Lecture Six in Michel Foucault, *The Hermeneutics of the Self* (Palgrave MacMillan, 2005).

2 February, Seoul

Revered sound and picture editor Walter Murch said that the length of a shot in a film should be the duration of time that you want the person to "think" that shot. (Compare Tarkovsky's *Nostalghia* to *The Hunger Games* then; the latter can't think.) This is also how I do paragraphs when I write. A paragraph is the length of time that I would like a reader to think the thought that is expressed in writing. Sometimes it's fifteen sentences, sometimes one.

18 February, Seoul

I stumbled across a video today on the problem of over-analysis in film studies and how it's ruining the enjoyment of movies. I don't agree with this conclusion, as there are many ways to enjoy a work of art and culture. But I do prefer to approach a film at the level of affect. I try to let myself go and take it as an experience, before doing any analysis. *How has it affected me?* is a far more salient outcome of a film than *What does it mean?* or *What does it represent?* This marks to me a key distinction between film analysis and film philosophy, and further, between the different practices of analyzing facts and philosophizing life. Too often, there is a presumption that a fact or series of facts lies in wait and needs to be put together to build what is *there* but not explicitly evident.

Specific to film, though, there are so many methods of writing and thinking through it because there is so much happening in the creation and unfolding. Filmmaking is *demiurgical*, creating a complex and chaotic stream of "life" that is then experienced for the life that is *made*. On some level, the demiurge knows what it means or what it expresses, but the images, signs, sounds, movements, actions, viewpoints, hearings also take on their own sense of expression. Further, a filmmaker works at an unconscious level, and further still, sometimes a filmmaker finds another stream along the way that was not planned and that stream emerges to the forefront. All of this is multiple, layered. This is how film takes on these qualities of thinking, dreaming and living, in process.

When I write about film, I try not to analyze. I can't uncover *what is there* and I have no interest in finding The Truth. I can only offer a way of thinking through what the film itself is expressing. This is also why I choose to do philosophy rather than theory. Theory builds upon its own analysis. I take things at this level of *expression*. I find something thematic in the film that helps a reader to think through this expression within this multiplicity that is somehow resonant in an interesting or ethical way. There are multiple truths to be drawn out from any expression, and this is as true of normal lived experience as a work of art.

I wish people writing about art would spend less energy analyzing works as if there is *something there*. Any fact houses a series of truths, and any series of facts houses a universe of activity impossible to reduce. Far better I think to appreciate that there are always many things going on in any *thing*, and there are many ways to creatively draw out something meaningful from it. After all, if there is one thing that it "says," then someone writing that is simply duplicating it in a less evocative form. At this point, who cares?

1 March, Kaohsiung

I'm listening to an infuriating podcast with civil rights lawyer Shahid Buttar. He's describing the problems of the Democratic Party's response to media disinformation, in which the party allies with media companies to control truth. On the question of speech/ censorship, the original intent of American liberalism was to combat misinformation with more information. This doesn't work in a digital age, and most certainly not in a Trumpist ecosystem in which information is amplified, scattered and proliferated through media corporations supported by and who support Democratic politicians. Some snippets I transcribed:[45]

"We're talking about companies controlling the organs of information—this is a bit of a stretch, but effectively brainwashing people. When you have Americans who are spoon-fed a version of a truth, we can't rely on the veracity of whatever that truth is as long as there aren't alternative narratives to combat it."

"You might think of our former president as a perfectly weaponized exploiter of the constitutional permissions that the founders built in. And I think Democrats are responding to the abuses of that system in a very linear fashion without recognizing the way in which the linear response creates a problem worse than what they're responding to."

"So Trump and right-wing media spreading disinformation is a problem. Having a single organ of truth deciding what is true and what is not, that everyone else would have to follow, is a problem far worse. That's stepping from Trump's world into Orwell's world, or perhaps Kafka's world where it's not even coherent."

"It's not just overcorrection for its own sake, it's overcorrection for the sake of corporate capital. And it's one thing to put corporate capital before people; it's an entirely different thing to put corporate capital not only before the interests of 300 million Americans, but also our constitutional framework. This is just one among many examples of how the bipartisan corporate congress is leading us into a ditch."

---

45 See *Useful Idiots* podcast dated February 27, titled "The Democrats Try to Cancel Fox News, with Shahid Buttar."

Today, media encompasses every aspect of our lives and it's promulgated through every institution we depend on, furthered by a new pandemic normal that has well prepared us to depend upon it, accept it, and live through it more than ever. We unquestionably live our lives *mediated*, in a way they couldn't imagine in the late 18th Century. Companies are supposed to thrive or fail based on our consumption of their products. Twitter, FB, Google... these aren't companies; they're legislators that we do not vote for, and which represent us based on their own interests.

I wish we could come to act on what is now so clear, that voting for Democrats enables and continues what Buttar is describing. There's so much wrong in this mass production of information-knowledge-belief proliferated through Facebook, Twitter, Google, et al. But one of the most ironic aspects to the story now unfolding is how much of its architecture was built through and continues to proliferate through the support of Clinton-Obama politicians. It's infected our very souls in every conceivable aspect of our thinking and living, exacerbated further by this pandemic normal that has functioned as a perfect training ground for our fearful minds.

10 March, Kaohsiung

Over this lonely and isolated year, I've been digging even more deeply than usual into readings. A theme of late is the attempt to tease out the distinctions between ancient Greek and Chinese traditions, not as a historical exercise but in drawing out the tendencies and habits that linger in today's thinking.

One aspect that keeps emerging is the concept of "purity." The Hellenistic era, transitioning from Stoic to Christian asceticism, is deeply embedded in purity. From Plato we are left with a concept of purity as existing outside of earthly attainment. We live only in its images and objects, the imitations (*mimesis*) of what is pure. From this we get God as transcendent, and we as imitations (poor ones) of his purity. Reaching toward purity is the *poiesis* of western creativity. It drives the individual to achieve greatness in art and thought. Ancient Chinese thinking doesn't have this. There is a variation of *mimesis*, but Asian philosophy and culture is about *immanence*: Nature, psyche and ethics flow into and inform each other.

The question that often resonates in my mind is this Nietszchean one of what we choose in a world without a single morality. I see patterns today of the continuing ancient Western unconscious. These Stoic/Christian concepts of purity have not left. The current pop-science consciousness of atheism and rationality have appropriated ancient purity in other expressions, other dogmas, other statements and images.

The internet brought a sea change that we're still grappling with. We are only a generation or so removed from a time when proximity and presence were our principal means of understanding, empathy, communication and community. We seem as a species to be poorly equipped to handle this shift. Information is in the bloodstream now. We think in information, we feel in information, we express and create under the gaze of information. We are unconsciously becoming informational creatures. It has affected every aspect of life, most prominently in this connection of education and work. Universities are training grounds for information processing.

What is different over the past 20 years or so, is that there has been a shift, thanks to the dominance of the internet and digital pervasiveness, from *poiesis* to criticism. The last two generations are being trained not to make things but to analyze things. We hear it everywhere—the supreme importance of facts, data, knowledge, reason and information. We isolate in order to cancel. We identify people by category. We package thought into answers and solutions. If

I'm right, that purity is embedded in the western soul, then it is no surprise that this version of purity does not apply practice (*praxis*) toward expression, but instead analyzes and criticizes toward closures. It's no surprise that we live in a world that battles over facts and identities, why we identify and cancel others, why we have become the panopticon, why we are the collective judges of morality. We atheists, having lost the need for a transcendent God, have taken up the mission to convert all to One Moral Purity.

What saddens me is the loss of art, the loss of expression, the loss of radicalism, the loss of courage, the loss of empathy. Purity today is entirely visual, adjudicated in a sea of statements and moving images. Analysis is not a writing but a "reading" of others, a textual analysis, a linear stream of commandments. It is a digital sampling of the human spirit. This atheist semiology extends to a purity in things, objects, images. Purity is objective—faith in the object and the representation. Purity is found in the fact. We are losing the ability to express, to feel, to sense, to intuit, to infer, to interpret, to suggest, to cast spells. We are theorists who have abandoned philosophy.

Another aspect of Nietzsche's work, and why I feel he is so important today, is the idea of "*ressentiment.*" Usually this is translated as "resentment," but key to his use is, from the French, a feeling, a reaction, a mental "sense" that gives a conscious response. It is an affective reaction given to thought and action. This resentment is not one side or another. It does not create, it reacts. This is our condition, our situation, our politics. We are entirely reactive. Nietzsche implores that the way to overcome resentment is to express, to affirm. But the way we think today—as digital, critical, informational, analytical—cannot affirm. It can only sample and react. Resentment, born of being affected, moves easily within a belief in one's rational processes—a belief in the purity of a process that is, in actuality, felt. In such a process, *ressentiment* itself becomes resent*ful*. This is the dark underbelly of today's liberalism.

A 21st Century purity requires little work. In the place of work is a demand to conform to language, to what is pure. The correction of language eliminates the need to think. This subservience to universal law is led by centrist liberals. Liberals of past generations were the makers of poetry, the makers of questions, the makers of openness. Now the liberal reacts out of resentment. For Nietzsche, when you react, that which you react to always sets the terms. Our reactions are oppositional, reinforcing the legitimacy of resentment. We all play in the same field, demanding closures from others, a new purity.

We are all men now.

10 April, Kaohsiung

The problem of this age is our thinking, how we think. It's a problem of method, thus a philosophical problem. What is created in thinking though our patterns of thought?

Strange that the problem is right before us. (What is more evident than that we think?) Not strange that we can't recognize it. (What is close is often what is most hidden.) The problem is a retention of dialectics and ontology in our discourse today. Ontology: the question of being, the question of what is. But in our age, it is answered in a name, a word, an identity. We are obsessing over what *is*. Dialectics: in the Platonic tradition, the method of opposition, contradiction and negation. This means that we are reactive rather than active. We identify what *is*, and if one says it is not, we counter by reifying what is. Such thinking is not creative. It adheres to essence and it plays at the level of *a priori* signification.

The problem is right before us because our age is viral. It cannot be seen, cannot be targeted, can barely be identified. Yet we react and identify. We enforce borders, we fast-track science to oppose, we shelter, quarantine, wait for what currently *is* to someday become what *is not*. We oppose biological life to biological death as the only measure of living.

We have not yet learned to become viral. To do so we would need to move along different processes of thought, ones that are not obsessed with *being*—its representational forms and its targeted solutions. Viral action and thought breaks out of identities and oppositions. It emerges and populates, gets under our skin, infects us, even threatening to sicken us. It doesn't care for what is. Virality finds expression in art, in lines and patterns that do not represent anything. Virality makes things unwell so that we may recover joy and beauty. Virality thrives through interaction, togetherness, infection. It is prone to error. It causes accidents. It experiments with uncertainty. It is particulate, mutable, transformational.

This virus, this horrible virus, cannot be *opposed*. We cannot content ourselves to simply react. We—our thinking, our art, our expressions—must become viral. We must produce and create beautiful viruses. We need to sing and laugh loudly together. To wait is to fear and cower. Only another, more rigorous, virality can overcome the virus that imprisons us in the protective shell of survival.

19 April, Kaohsiung

The difference between conspiracy and philosophical inquiry is one of answer versus question. It is a decision to answer or a decision to question. Conspiracy decides that what may be incidental is in fact purposeful. Nihilism decides that what may be purposeful is incidental.

Inquiry does neither. Inquiry suspends the answer to continue the question. This is difficult to do in contemporary mediated discourses, which are dominated by the proliferation of (and demand for) answers to overcome doubt. Answers are provided by the authority of facts, science and specialists. Science and conspiracy follow the same process, for which we are all well trained: arrange the evidence, make connections, follow what makes sense, hypothesize and conclude. It is the DIY/bootstraps ideal of USA frontierism nudged into the architecture of the information/science psyche. Conspiracy is one logical outcome of American ideology.

Inquiry is different in that it has not yet concluded. (Science used to thrive on inquiry, but in its financial and ideological alliance with State interests, it usually conforms to State mandates.) Inquiry maintains the value of uncertainty, an ethics of living anarchy. Our problem is not a lack of reason; we are all acting under a belief in our own reasoning. Our solution is not more information, more technology, more science. Our way out is the way of the warrior—to strip away the noise that proliferates so that one may listen to the shifting breeze, to unsee what is present so that one may scan the horizon, to equip oneself, to relearn how to linger in other thinking.

4 May, Kaohsiung

A "white man moment" is when a white man reposts a "person of color moment" of a "white woman moment."

16 May, Kaohsiung

We can think of *life* itself as the time which passes—call it objective time, ontological time—the time as itself which is experienced in its durations of various lived speeds and lengths and overlaps. We can think of *conceptual thought*, philosophy included, as clock and calendar time. Time as itself, experienced in its passing, has neither clock nor calendar. It is life, lived experience, the chaos of life. Time as clock and calendar is a means of dividing time into manageable and predictable units of ordering. It enables us to turn time into a *reference*. This composes and conceives a different objectivity, not time as itself but time as we render it *into an object*. This is where a word such as "objectivity" fails in its purity.

Back to the point: Time lived by clock and calendar is an abstraction of time, a division into manageable units of seconds, minutes, hours, days, weeks, months, seasons and years. Time as itself is lived. It has no precise divisions. It is seasonal.

The distinction of lived and clock/calendar time marks on the one hand a distinction of life and philosophy. Life moves of its own accord and we live both *as* it and *within* it. We conceptualize and explain life using something like a metaphorical clock.

Ancient philosophers made their own clock-like reductions of nature and cosmos: Thales' water, Heraclitus' "*logos*," etc. In the 2,500 years that followed, new thinkers revised or remade the image of what all these various instruments of thought were. But even as recent as 50 years ago, they never removed life from the model. The two were joined to produce the concept.

Philosophy over the past two generations has changed. As scholarship becomes more institutionalized in today's academia, scholars merely *reference* existing clock and calendar models. One is only allowed to write if one is able to first explain the intricacies of the metaphorical clock or calendar under study. And from there, one tends merely to "paint it in a new light" or "re-situate it" for today, or to apologize for the errors of the picture of the clock that have led us astray. No one is bothering to question the increments. Why seconds, minutes and hours? Why days? Is this really how time functions?

The distinction of lived and clock/calendar time is not only academic. This kind of scholarship, this informational and fact-driven explanatory tendency, has infiltrated our daily social discourses, online and in person. With every advancement in mechanistic, technological, automated, informational thinking, we become more clock and calendar and less alive. Even a *fact*, so desired in today's liberal discourses, is a unit of life that is extracted from the lived flow and used to express a truth of life. A fact is nothing more than 16 May 2021 at 07:55. It is a reference point for the future and the past, one used to draw out a fixed entity from the flow that passed through it. The problem is that we do not recognize this distinction. As we fail in this, the clock and calendar *replace* what is lived time. This is the logical advancement of reason in an age of information. Today it feels as though lived time is equivalent to clock time, or worse, that the fact is preserved while the experience is forgotten. It seems as if memory only has value if the recollection can be isolated, documented, and validated.

This is what happens when creativity is being eviscerated in favor of the stacking of accurate and functional data points. Creativity requires the continuance of the very imprecision of lived time. There is no vitality in the *mechanism* of time, only precision. *Vitalism*, a word so derided today, moves though time devoid of prior divisions and reference points. Creativity has functions—it sees ends, it achieves goals. But it thrives best in its unsettled state of newness and openness, a striving and flourishing unconstrained by references, identities and categories. Creativity is not the place of being something, it is an act that becomes something.

23 May, Kaohsiung

The increased restrictions on movement by State mandates are pushing my thoughts increasingly into the philosophical problem of "control," and within this, related ideas of power, compliance, expression, and freedom. These are all difficult ideas, all unanswerable ideas that are interconnected but also distinct. Everyone seems to be discussing biology as the problem of our time. We are paying little attention to the effect of this—the collisions of control and compliance—as we negotiate the future of freedom. I mean freedom both in the sense of biology (one's body) and thought (one's ideas). The danger of noncompliance is the loss of human life. The danger of compliance is the risk of habituation against freedom and expression. By danger, I mean this interplay of "life" and "living" —they're not the same thing and they are very much in tension.

I don't read much fiction. I'm not very good at it. But this interest in the present and future of control (life) and expression (living) led me to take another stab. I've never read *Brave New World* or *1984*. I know they're often compared, and that their language and concepts are frequently referenced without considering their origin. I've used "Orwellian" in conversation, having only read *Animal Farm* several times. But I don't really know what that means.

So, in spurts between my normal philosophy readings that I do, I found time over the past few months to slowly read both novels. I read the Huxley first, since it's older, then Orwell. What follows are some thoughts on both, and what they might have to say in regard to this tension of control and expression. (I should add that I haven't read any analysis of their comparison, aside from a brief section in Wikipedia about the two books; I'm trying to keep to my own readings.)

What you have in both novels are two very different ideas on the future of control societies. Having read both, I now see their influence in so many of the films I've already seen and thought to be brilliantly original. There are way too many to mention, but films like *THX1138, One Flew Over the Cuckoo's Nest* and *The Matrix* got repeated play in my imagination while reading both novels, as did several episodes of *Star Trek*. In *BNW*, control is achieved through the manipulation of desire. In *1984*, control is achieved through the codification of language. *BNW* describes a society drugged by "soma," which brings a surface-level joy that eliminates the desire to do anything against the state of control in which compliance *makes sense*. Why rebel, why question, why think differently, why go against this wonderful peace and calm? There's simply no good reason to do so. *1984* is a world of managed acceptance of the benevolence and care, indeed even the "love," of the State (Big Brother). Language and memory are the key devices in the management of thought and knowledge.

I preferred *1984* to *BNW*. It's not close for me. First, I found Orwell the superior writer, the deeper writer, the more thought-provoking writer. I enjoyed (and sympathized with) the two central characters more than anyone in *BNW*. Huxley is the more subtle writer. He read to me as more playful, even sardonic at times; if it were told orally, I'd imagine the rhapsode wearing a wry, British smile. It's also a bit silly in some of its world-building, like a sci-fi TV show from the 1960s. By contrast, Orwell is dead serious, and his world-building is timeless. *1984* is a horrific novel. There was no "holy shit" moment for me in *BNW*. *1984* had several, but in particular: The outcome of Winston's experience in Room 101, *what he said*, floored me. Perhaps I was more engaged in Orwell's story, where I found myself more distracted in Huxley's. This is not an objective analysis, this paragraph, it's personal taste.

Which then is the more resonant novel for 2021? Both. As we scan the horizon of impending control, each novel brings its own set of warnings. Taken together they provide a complementary mix. I can't say that one is "more important" or "more likely" because there's nothing in either to definitively argue (or argue against). These are brilliant seers. Our concern of the moment is an amalgamation of the key ideas in both texts. The future danger is a world in which people are pacified by a narrow satisfaction while at the same time in a state of anxiety about going against the terms of universal thought. They are complimentary forms of conditioning, leading to a singularity of conviction. I found it particularly interesting that in Orwell, the method was to *reduce* rather than add to language—that is, to reduce the available signifiers in the English lexicon. This effectively reduces the risk of ambiguity and interpretation in language. This, not surprisingly, results in a world in which art is compliant to the interests of the collective, which is to say, the State. Couple this with the pacification of Huxley's soma and the narrowing of possible *experience* and you have a version of our very possible near future. What is different in our future—unimaginable in Huxley or Orwell— is that the State is us, the world we ourselves are producing.

If I had read both in 2000, I might say that Huxley better describes the dystopia to come. We had the internet as our means of pleasure. We could see then the mollifying effect it would come to have. You could even draw this forward another 10 years. We pet our rectangles and achieve desire gratification from the endless stream of images and statements, a stream that provides no story, no closure, no ethics, no conclusion, no idea to carry away. Huxley was right. Our technology today is our soma. He was also very keen to present a situation in which there is nothing to overturn, no axis point of possible change. Orwell's control invites the possibility of rebellion, which is indeed present in the novel. I'll give props to Huxley here, but even in Orwell's world, it would be extraordinarily difficult to organize. Plato's Cave is an effective allegory here. In both novels, to overcome you'd have to literally *change your mind.*

If I read Orwell in 2000, I'd say "No way, never gonna happen." But in 2021, in the aftermath of Trump, in the rise of Xi, with the technology we have and the virus that refuses to leave, it's very possible. Orwell was working through a post-WWII environment in which the threat of communism was a real concern. The world managed to stave this off and it dissolved as a threat after the Cold War. The threat now is not just nations, but how nations that overtly apply control produce an ambience of global reactiveness to it. And if we are reacting to it, we subconsciously legitimize it. If control works for those nations, it becomes a weapon for other nations as well. This is the effect of current CCP policies on the USA mindset—they work. The arms race of today is not the atom bomb, it's the efficacy of systems. Control is now dominant in nations around the world.

The political problem in *1984* is not limited to Oceania (UK/USA); every alliance/nation has its own control because the methods have no borders. The mechanisms and psychology of control have spread like a virus. This is one of the most terrifying and visionary aspects of Orwell's world. There is no *them*—except as a means of drumming up nationalism—every government employs the same means. This nationalism of "them" masks the fact that all societies share the same methods. Taking this to what we are conditioned to view as a liberal/conservative divide, the US is like two nations employing different methods of the same thing. Media programming produces the psychology that this is the correct thought to have against the other, ignoring that the structure of power is built off of this otherness that is, at an *essential* level, the same. As in Orwell, we find at the global level, the CCP and USA exchanging, even if unconsciously, the strategies of adaptation of the other in the manufacturing of systems. Because our control is made through compliance within a global technological architecture, no borders are necessary. We are the managers of our condition.

This is the chilling thing. It is an extension of what is evident in both novels. Even though the State manages society, each presents the threat not as an external force, but as something that lives inside the mind. (Orwell exceeds Huxley in playing with the psychology of inside and outside, self and other.) This is something we fail to grasp today. Science is a legitimate practice. But our conditioning of science-thought conceives a problem as outside of us. "I am rational," is the inner voice of every person; "the threat is outside of me, it's everyone else." This thinking pervades our discourses in 2021. The problem is that "I am rational" is, as Huxley and Orwell show, easily manipulable by the technology of progress, the brave new world, that we've consumed and celebrated. "I am rational" is malleable. It is the weapon of conformity. Contrary voices on any subject today are easily dismissed, ridiculed, cast aside as irrational. "Follow the science," we say. OK. But "science" is faith in the work that scientists do. Often, the counter to science is dismissed as conspiracy. But conspiracy is not brainwashing, conformity is. Conspiracy is opening to possibility, but it's fueled by fear and lack of awareness. It's the ignorant cousin to free expression and radical ideas. The problem is we're casting out the latter with the former in order to preserve and conform to the universal order of control.

"Just for now," we say. OK. But we're planting the infrastructure for control by our conformity. *We're making the world right now.* Our mental pathways are changing—our habits, our faith, our thresholds of acceptance. It's happening now. The manufactured divide in the US of liberal/conservative ignores that we encourage this divide through our codification of correctness. It is a mass condition that everyone participates in. It is not reserved to the United States. Globally, we have canceled art and expression for the interests of correctness as a morality of control. Art—*real* art, the production of *newness*—is the only means of breaking control. History has shown this. But it is being actively suppressed right now. Everyone is participating in the necessity of control. We need to nurture an ethics of expression and the wildness of living to overcome the control of "bare life." We need a publicness that is not mediated by corporations allied with governments. We need to sing again.

29 May, Kaohsiung

The very public "I got the jab" social media posting bothers me. I believe people's hearts are in the right place. In one sense, it communicates unity and positivity, and is a sign for others to follow suit and join the chorus so we can all get through this together. Because I am not in the States, and only see it through software, I'm failing to see the terror that's rattling my birth home. I imagine this divide among close friends and family, believing this invisible terror to be different things that engender different responses. Perhaps the social display is one of love.

But the message is not just a message to another person. As social, it is given to *all*, and as such is passive, indeed passive-aggressive. As given to all, the sign is also an expression of new power. This is not the top-down law of State control, but the individual as a *representation* of control (a symbol). The sign is the smiling logic of conformity that replaces the hard power of explicit law. It *feels* like an act of free will, but it's siphoned down one stream of thought through the mechanisms of government, science and corporate wealth. I don't mean that wealth is the *intention,* but its solution is a benefit gained by a profit-based public health institution. The smile shared with the public is a sign of relief and community; but it's also a sign of pharmaceutical profit, an expression of its validity. Signs are always multiple, even as they aim to be singular. This is how semiotics works. The smile is a *semiotic* affirmation of the *real* intersection of these multiple expressions of power.

Another thing that bothers me is the privilege of it. The jab-and-smile communicates a sign that one lives in a narrow society of economic advantage, while most of the world does not. The vaccinated have benefitted from being free from global political mechanisms that are occurring, for example, in parts of Asia. The western world is hoarding, and the jabbed are flaunting this privilege. Some people don't want the jab, but many can't even get it.

Perhaps the greatest concern is that this seems to be a manifestation of a general, widespread attitude of acceptance to control as an expression of conformity. Setting aside the virus and vaccine for a moment, this collision of control and conformity is emerging into a global zeitgeist. It's something Asian nations have long lived with, but it's relatively new to North America and North Europe. This reverse flow of globalization—the importing of Chinese solutions to overcome chaotic situations—is a recent subconscious state for the West. It has been happening gradually over the past decade. As CCP solutions work, American utilitarianism takes notice.[46] This is reflected in education, economics, censorship, and the attempt to corral thought into single solutions. This isn't the first time the USA has managed its states of exception. But it is the first to be influenced by digital ubiquity and global awareness, and socially propagated by the "free will" gesture of conformity.

It may turn out to be the greatest harm of Trumpism is yet to come—that in his aftermath, a devotion to the Good State takes its place. Revolutionary dialectics often do this: A strong, ostensibly Bad State is replaced by another strong, ostensibly Good State, wherein the latter maintains the essence of the former. In the case of Trump, his *opposition*, his reaction, takes on many of the same strategies. The result is a continuance of Trumpism as the new idea that installed the dialectic. In post-Trump Trumpism, what we find are displays of

---

[46] When I criticize "China," I'm criticizing, in one sense the Chinese Communist Party, but more specifically, the US legitimization of CCP-style thought-control without naming it as such. This is not a criticism of Chinese culture or people.

strong-State allegiance that are antithetical to (while maintaining the essence of) the previous strong-State allegiance:

1. Social media posts flaunting stickers and shoulders, etc.

2. This new rule that jabbed kids can go without masks while un-jabbed kids must wear masks. This is a visible sign of compliance to the State, using children no less. (Materially, this rule makes no sense, as everyone should be wearing masks; it is rather a political move, a coercive sign of the Good State that is anti-Trump.)

3. An increase, rather than a decrease, in shaming and intolerance I see for oblique points of view on anything against the State.

4. A growing lack of any kind of resistance to conformity. We are experiencing a severe drought in artistic resistance outside of identifiable issues of race, gender and sexuality.

5. How corporate media has become fully compliant to government messages under the name of "science." It is not only news media, but advertising, PSAs, celebrity statements, etc.

It's all compliance. One could argue it's all *correct*, even though the plainest of all truths is that *we do not know what we're doing*. We're reacting out of fear and an idea of logic. We're exhausted, exhausted from Zoom faces, from families sheltered in close quarters, from losing the vital element of "play" in our lives. We are collectively realigning our minds right now, conditioning ourselves toward the future. What kind of world are we shaping through this conformity?

Maybe it's me. Maybe it's the books I read. Maybe I and all my friends are just old. People are worried about their children and stressed about the Republican other. But *in my day* (shakes walking stick) we resisted government as a means of changing it. Now the center-left (the left with money) is in compliance with social norms and the directives of the state. The accusation that progressives are regressive rings true. Maybe it's simply that the Middle has won, that centrism feeds the needs of this day. Republicans are composed of a bizarre alliance of corporate shareholders and home owners enjoying their white supremacy, plus jobless, working-class traditionalists afraid of losing their notion of white supremacy. Democrats are a party that isolates its leftist elements against itself (Nietzsche's division of forces). True progressivism and rebellion is pitted *against* media-literate centrist snobs and culture warriors earning six figure salaries. This Middle is firmly in control and they are now in the advantaged position of being a member of the Media-State alliance. Biden's Democrats have no incentive to question anything the government says. They are *reacting* as an expression of *ressentiment*.

I'll always stand with the free thinkers and the artists over the conformists and the rationalists. The former incite change. They affirm. The latter bide their time until they can safely and comfortably die.

2 June, Kaohsiung

Rhetoric is interesting. It is the method, the delivery, the means of argument, and the thing said. Some people have mad rhetorical skills. It's funny to me how pastors, preachers and other such proselytizers enunciate words to dismiss an otherwise harmless word. I just stumbled upon a preacher named Voddie Baucham, who addresses valuable points in Critical Race Theory.[47] He applies the rhetorical technique of elongating an otherwise valid word in order to invalidate it. It's another tactic of institutional power to preserve itself. He, a black man, is effectively preserving the dogma he belongs to (Christianity). When he speaks, and the way in which he speaks,

---

[47] See https://youtu.be/xuSMvIVtd0A.

makes sense. The authority is not so much the ideology itself, rather that the institution grants him a position of authority.

That said, I like the way he broke CRT into four main arguments. And it reminds me why I'm conflicted. I have problems with "theory" anyway, with its analytical and linguistic gamesmanship, and its tendency to destroy one set of principles to supplant them with another. Theory, steeped in Marxism, is reactive. I disagree with points 1 and 2 for this reason. I feel CRT is doing the same kind of narrowing that is expressed by the speaker, proclaiming an essence to every expression. It's neither accurate nor helpful for creating more equal and just societies, but it does make the NYT best-seller list.

Conversely, I'm totally on board with points 3 and 4. These are the less theoretical and more philosophical streams. Here CRT is seeking out "other knowledge" and minority expressions, which have the capacity to shake existing dogmas. What the pastor here gets wrong is his notion of "objective truth." Jordan Peterson makes the same mistake. Postmodernism and the Frankfurt School do not claim that there are no objective truths, but that truth is a function of power. That is, truth comes through assemblages of power, not the other way around. This is a philosophical approach to power, describing its means of preservation but also its ability to express new lines of thought from out of the canon of knowledge and history. This is the more therapeutic and affirmational line to run with. But we'd need a branching of CRT into something else—another name without the C or the T, something more philosophical.

5 June, Kaohsiung

I'm reading Hannah Arendt's seminar notes from 1955.[48] Totalitarianism sees subjects as living animals. In regarding such a subject, there is only life and death. Outside of this practical matter lies all the varieties of living, worldly, sensual relationships. A logical container of life and death has no world, only "body versus body, life against life, corpse against corpse." This leads to a collapse of reality and a descent into nightmarish outcomes.

• Loneliness arises out of this condition, a loss of world and a loss of self.

• Authority is always separated from self, something outside the self; it always has an imperative, always "in the name of..."

• To be oneself one needs a world, an environment, and other people in it; in absence of a world, ideology takes hold, the dangerous isolation of thought and ideas.

• Orwell: We become "domesticated animals," which are worse than animals; incapable of action; "we would only react to varying circumstances and our consciousness would only be the registrar of whatever happens to us"; being safe, getting fed, etc.

I'm modifying her a little with these points, but the spirit of her critique and concern resonates.

---

[48] See "Hannah Arendt papers: 1898-1977," available on the Library of Congress website at: https://hdl.loc.gov/loc.mss/eadmss.ms001004.

9 June, Kaohsiung

Facebook is a super-ego-generating machine: the production of authority upon and within the subject. From this is projected an appearance of morality as subjects. From the Facebook super-ego mechanism, the ego goes to work: one gets to curate one's own illusion of free thought as a means to preserve oneself against the chaos of infinity. No wonder we're so aggressive toward those allied to other illusions. We remain unconscious to the fact that I and the other are both being produced to serve the same unapparent master: the God that streams the thought-binary and manifests the illusion of oneself.

15 June, Kaohsiung

Describing history as "conditional" is an acknowledgement of how power has produced its course. We commonly regard history as a "series of key events" assembled as a string of causal occurrences that produce a narrative. But to regard history as conditional is to recognize that there is something other than the events, which underlies the story. This "something" is multiple and difficult to name. History as conditional means that the relations of events are not only to each other but also that *their* relations are relational to the very conditions of history. This is the heart of the concept of *genealogy*, as Nietzsche proposed and Foucault advanced. Behind the narrative of history lie the conditions of power that pushed the dominant myth.

One "something" we can name, among many somethings, is white supremacy or male supremacy as the dogma that advances the dominant narrative. The experiences of non-white-males are the other stories that lived the condition but which do not advance the historical narrative. To diagnose only the white and male events identifies facts but ignores the stickiness of the sediment or the soil that nurtures and enables them. Science works in a similar manner. The study of any phenomena requires knowing, in advance, the legitimate research—its narrative. It can only test under a linear stream of functional data to extract the datum of knowledge.

To view history as conditional is different from the work of a dialectician, who would enter and see oppositions, identities, contrasts and contradictions. A diagnostician is different from a dialectician. The diagnostician of a condition identifies not any things in opposition but the condition itself as the sickness to be cured. A diagnostician of history recognizes the sickness not as material but as psychological. The condition is a psychology of dialectics *as* the illness, not as a means of change. Dialectics is the problematic condition, the psychological problem of history that continues. In other words, we all are *all* produced through the lingering dialectics of white and male thought, ideas and structures of power and discipline. A dialectician thinks in a kind of generalized science that pulls out from experience this *or* that thing to analyze toward the attainment of knowledge. A diagnostician of history recognizes that the condition of dialectics as a method is the very problem of history.

We see this playing out with the growing vaccine imperative. Scientifically, universal vaccination makes perfect sense. But there is a genealogy to this, another history of people of color who are resistant to the vaccines for reasons that are highly complicated (as genealogies are). This is a story untold, unregarded for history, because it doesn't work within the white-dominant science of the vaccines. The dialectic of white pro-vax and white anti-vax is the only story being rendered for history.

It's difficult to use language and thought in other non-dialectical ways because language itself is made to reproduce oppositions, negations, vision, objects, acquisition, information, etc. Through this we are all conditioned. To overcome this, we need to start thinking history as conditional and psychological to challenge the problems of power.

The above statement is perhaps better composed in a *logic*, such as:

<u>Proposition 1</u>. White (European) and male supremacy is the dominant condition of history. The structures of discourse, morality, laws, concepts, sciences, technology, aesthetics, religion and other institutional disciplines we have today are the product of white and male dominance. This is the conscious reality of historical events.

<u>Proposition 2</u>. P1 composes the material and unconscious condition that underlies all "western" thought. This can be named as "white supremacy" and "patriarchy." This is the "condition"—that is, the unconscious psyche underlying the consciousness of events in their causal progression.

<u>Proposition 3</u>. P1 was historically and consciously celebrated, and P2 unconsciously regaled on supremacist grounds (birthright, biology, "nature," etc.).

<u>Proposition 4</u>. Over the past few generations, the virtues of P1-P3 have been increasingly called into question for subjugating minority rights/justice and dismissing minority contributions to history.

These four propositions together lead in today's discourses to the following dialectical responses...

<u>Response A</u>. A "nature" reactive opposition. This response *negates* the stated criticisms of P4, which are viewed as a discursive threat to whiteness and maleness—the dominant ideology. In other words, RA consciously opposes the *discourse* of P4 to empower the material *reality* of P1-P3. The method of opposition is usually presented on *natural* grounds.

Response B. A "culture" reactive opposition. This *asserts* the realities of P1-P3, which leads to oppositional methods of enhancing power in the opposite direction. In other words, RB opposes RA by negating RA's power. RB is referred to colloquially as "woke" and is argued on *cultural* grounds.

Effect: Both RA and RB are dialectical. RA opposes/ contradicts the discursivity of P4 to protect the material supremacy of P2. RB affirms the discursivity of P1-P4 by negating the RA opposition to P4.

Conclusion 1: Dialectical opposition by both methods discursively preserves the material reality of P1-P3.

Rationale: RA and RB are what we find conjoined and playing out in capitalist, profit-based media dialectics. It produces two oppositional sides, each of which aims to become the dominant power. Social media imitates the strategies of capitalist-media oppositions. It trains people to reproduce, copy, and identify oppositions through dialectical language. This reactionary strategy confirms the power of RA that negates the power RB, or confirms the power of RB by negating RA.

Strategies of RA and RB in action:

They express mainly through alliances in the production of memes and symbols: flags, hats, banners, slogans, hashtags, etc. RA negates through bad information, rousing hateful tendencies, appealing to racist fears, etc. RB negates through canceling and shaming, which neuters artistic expression; it morally negates as a means of purifying its affirmation. All of this enlivens opposition itself. The main beneficiary of the opposition is the one dominant power, which is capitalist power. Such power exists outside of these discourses, but its products of news media and social media content and technology profit from RA and RB engaging in the unresolvable dialectic. RA and RB in action benefit corporate wealth and exacerbate anxiety among consumers and participants.

<u>Proposition 5</u>. While P1 and P2 compose the dominant conditions of power and oppression, such power has developed through a neglect and active suppression of the contributions of "minoritarian" ideas, discourse, ethics, aesthetics, actions, language, science, etc.[49] This is historical.

<u>Proposition 6</u>. Minoritarian ideas compose "alternate" or "other" expressions that help to creatively unsettle the dominant power. "Minoritarian" refers to any expression that is "other than" P1, whether that comes through another race, gender, situation, act or expression. This is strategic and active.

<u>Proposition 7</u>. While P1 composes the conditions and psychology of P2 power, P6 advances non-oppositional, non-binary, non-dialectical expressions as a different power, a power of *difference*.

Such non-dialectical, minoritarian strategies would be something like...

<u>Response C</u>. To be critical (of the discourse of both RA *and* RB).

<u>Effect</u>: Being critical of RA and RB is to be critical of their strategies, not their essences. It recognizes that the discursive strategy of opposition is itself the problem.

<u>Response D</u>. To be affirmational (to create "another" expression).

<u>Effect</u>: This other is a non-binary. It aims to produce something new in thought and action. This is the Nietzsche-

---

[49] "Minoritarian" is a term used by Deleuze and Guattari. I am applying the term to specifically advocate the inclusion of "becoming-minoritarian" expressions, against the imposition of an identity-power opposition.

Deleuze productive force of artistic expression, new ideas, tragedy, and joyful affirmations.

Conclusion 2: RC and RD escape dialectical opposition/ negation to advance the production of positive, progressive change.

Rationale: RC and RD, criticism and expression, are not oppositional-to P1 and P2; they are other-than P1 and P2. They produce new ideas outside the opposition upon which capitalist media thrives.

Strategies of RC and RD in action:

RC is something not many people are doing because it risks the RB accusation of non-alliance. This accusation comes when one is incapable of thinking outside of mediated dialectics. RC must fight against both this reduction and the RA reduction. Rather than upholding the dialectic through alliances, the RC strategy aims to be critical of the one power (rather than dual oppositions) and those whose language of opposition upholds it.

RD, meanwhile, is the production of new art and new strategies of thought. This is the aspect of BLM and OWS whose supporters are actually out in the streets and producing new thought, ideas, events, crises, stories and other expressions—in defiance of reductions to fixed, media-generated language. It is also found in non-dialectical, expansive writing such as poetry and storytelling, and through music, theater, photography, and other artistic expressions. This again is a Nietzschean production of ideas that is active and affirmational, not reactive.

19 June, Kaohsiung

I'm back to re-engaging Deleuze's *Difference and Repetition,* which has become such a massive influence on how I think the world around me.

Deleuze doesn't waste words. Right from the start, he describes the problem of philosophy, which is really the problem of discourse and how we think our relationships with each other and our concepts of truth. His opening is a defense of "difference." Philosophical history subordinates difference to identity (in order to think it), to resemblance (in order to understand/communicate our perception of something), to opposition (to establish predicates, to produce a binary), and to analogy (in order to judge). All are attempts at reduction for the purposes of repeating sameness, found not only in science and communication, but all aspects of life. If we can say one thing about discourse in 2021 it is: identify, contain, name, judge and communicate.

This is our lingering Greek mind, our dialectical programming that has become mastered through the European tradition of education and overall learning. We reproduce sameness and identity through our unconscious mastery of such methods. Our expertise in rhetorical dialectics allows us to engage in the identification of opposites, contradictions, and dualities of affirmation and negation.

That's me editorializing Deleuze. He doesn't do such critiques. Instead he wants to offer an affirmational (non-dialectical) practice of drawing out difference from the processes of life and thought. Difference is a means of creatively circumventing identity, representation, opposition and analogy. With difference as the point of emphasis, life opens up its possibilities for other thought and action. Difference repeats (life) and we repeat difference (in thought, action, living).

Deleuze doesn't oppose but *resists* dialectics. He instead works in pairs. In the former, there is a "being," seemingly or nominally identifiable. Through practices of contradiction, negation and opposition, comes the development or advancement of the idea from it. In Deleuze's pairs, there is one thing or event in the process of formation and activity, plus something else that is also real; they do not reside in opposition. Often, this something else evades notice and has not earned the right of appearance or discursive value. As the one repeats so does the other, but the differential element—that which produces the life and action of the event—lies in the movement of the other, which can only emerge in *signs*.

Deleuze uses various terms and personae for this other, generative, unseen activity: intensive processes, a dark precursor, Dionysus. It is the other (minoritarian) expression also underway as the majority of X versus Y (or X vs not-X) plays itself out. The majority composes truth in any area of lived experience: political argument, historical record, categorical identification, law, science, religion, rhetorical gamesmanship. We are trained to believe in the virtue of one side against another, but instead, the dialectic itself *is* the power. (Extend this to news media and social media discourse and you see the problem: we are exacerbating our powerlessness by inflating the power of the oppositional/identity mechanism itself; this can be extended as well to voting and other easily resolvable situations.)

Deleuze's method is Nietzschean; it is an ahistorical genealogical process, describing an ongoing activity of powers and forces that underlie known structures. This is not paranoia, it is an act of tracing the immanent reality of processes that defy identification. Beyond "Good" and "Evil" lie forces that gather and assemble. The ethics here is that in one sense, such forces work to declare the nominal validity of one or the other. But in a more positive sense, these assemblages of power are capable of breaking the majority rule through creative work that expresses the joys of life and all its possibilities. These "expressions" move outside of, or other than, identities and representations.

This is also a way of rethinking a range of ideas in activism and creative arts. Take racial injustice as an example. Right now, CRT is the Big Conversation in news media. We find a pro- and an anti-side; we see a definition of terms, claims of truth versus counter-truth, etc, etc. Magnifying the power of the *minority group* sets up an oppositional and contradictory relation, which in hypermediated discourses creates antagonism. Further, such reactionary politics benefits the mechanism of power, the media consumptive machine, by containing the identities of discourse.

Magnifying instead the power of the *minoritarian expression* opens to a repetition of difference as another way, a way that unsettles majority thought, i.e. the fixed, unconscious condition of white supremacy. This is why BLM was so important, why OWS was so important. They were, in the early days anyway, expressions without terms. What we have to work against is not the other side, but rather the mechanism as a whole that produces sides of division for its own capitalist benefit. The quickest way to destroy a movement is to set the terms of discourse. This moves what is expressed into what is mediated. Once mediated, it is identified and thus easy to oppose.

The distinction here is an ethics of resistance rather than revolution. Revolution is based on an opposition by one nameable, identifiable slogan of forces or allied sides. Resistance is underway when someone recognizes that something is wrong and devises a creative strategy to usurp it. I see ethics when one subverts the universal command to obey the majority and to conform to what we identify as the correct thing to do. My heart jumps a little when I see a police video of a motorcyclist going on a joyride and evading police. Is he doing the wrong thing, putting lives at risk? Sure. But he's also taking a risk to experience this one expression of pure freedom. For this hour of his life, he has defied the universal mandate. In the process, he has truly lived in a way that this new liberalism of our time is draining from our souls.

When enough people gather to resist, and to resist being named and identified for the corporate discourse, these instances modify the whole. This concept of modification is evident in Deleuze, through his readings of Bergson. But it is also Spinozan: if the expression is joyful, if it affirms, if it is different, habits become broken and change becomes possible.

22 June, Kaohsiung

Those who are ambitious, who strive for higher goals in their careers, are the ones most enslaved to the demands of labor. I see this particularly amplified in the States and in Asia. With technological ubiquity, people don't have work hours, they work continually— constantly "in reach," constantly giving themselves to whatever company/institution they labor for. This leads to high stress and mental/physical unhealth. It also means that work wins over the human need for lingering and leisure. Work as labor means the work always wins. We constantly labor because we convince ourselves that the work we're doing is important. The purpose of living becomes something deferred, abstracted from the presence of lived experience, that purpose being the personal accumulation of enough wealth to eventually stop laboring.

What if instead we decided that our work was unimportant, that it is ancillary to an otherwise good life? This doesn't mean that we do shitty work or stop doing projects; it means that the labor of work is limited, becoming an aspect of life in service to something outside of ourselves. In a way, this describes what work is, something given to the world. But techno-capitalism has convinced the individual of the importance of the individual as a means of nurturing the health of the company. This is how cult-like allegiances form around one's company.

It extends as well to independent workers—"gig workers" and "digital nomads." The only difference here is the production of a narcissist bubble in which the individual is *also* the company. A cult of one, enslaved to one's own labor, producing a cycle of in(ner-)dependence. To amend Arendt's *vita activa* equation for today: Work is the work one does; labor is what one gives or sacrifices to something outside oneself (the state or the company). The ambitious nomad chooses to gain freedom from the forces outside the self. But such a worker risks becoming enslaved to the self, laboring for the ambitious self.

But in techno-capitalism, the work has also changed the labor. If I'm a carpenter (consider that a placeholder profession), I take value in my work, I see directly the result of what I make, I don't have to answer a text message at 11pm about arranging a meeting about the status of a report on new data about the feasibility of the cabinet I'm working on; I don't have to concern myself with whether this cabinet is compliant with version 2.2.03 software that will be out of date in three months. I could instead work on this cabinet—this one here in front of me, right now—and when I'm not, I could go home to my family, be with them here in front of me, right now, and not have to dwell on the impossible array of anxieties as I'm falling asleep at night. I could live my life distinct from my labor.

That's not to say that being a "carpenter" would be easy or stress free. But I surely would be free from the complexity of psychosomatic anxiety streams that an "intelligent" profession demands. This is the flip that has occurred in contemporary techno-capitalism: the high-income earners are the ones constantly enslaved to the demands and expectations of others, feeding a machinery whose wealth is distributed to those who exist outside of the toils of constant labor. Worse still, this conformity to corporate labor today demands proof of one's allegiance. It chills me that in Taiwan, emails about administrative matters in my field of academia are sent around 1am. This signifies one's willing conformity to the demands of the institution, that one is ambitious, that one is willing to always be working. The high earners, the ambitious, and the most active are the ones with the least amount of freedom.

1 July, Kaohsiung

Unresolved thought of the morning: in English, the concepts "memory" and "the imagination." Why does imagination get the article "the" but memory does not?

Philosophical history treats memory as some kind of subjective container or field of the past that *repeats*, while the imagination is an active function that *makes*. Memory is experience, while imagination is considered one operation ("the") that is done with the mind.

But they feed on each other. Recent cognitive science suggests the two faculties have far more in common than they are different. Imagination is nothing without memory; but any thinking of memory is imagined. "The memory" is an active organ that actualizes thought through an act of imagining.

That is to say, everything you think you know about yourself is imagined. Knowledge of the self is a poetic act.

Or maybe the reason is more colloquial and common, a function of language to reduce ambiguity. "The" memory, or "a" memory, is a specific instance, which would be better named "a recollection." But that doesn't explain imagination. "The imagination" is never one thing: "Wow, *that imagination* was really something!" It's almost like the latter is some kind of malady, a fantasy or fiction, never granted the status of being real.

3 July, Kaohsiung

I was reminded over this morning's coffee, once again, of times of travel and openness. People who are sedentary can't understand, but the lives that so many of us have cultivated living outside of our birthplace is nomadic. Over time, nomadicism becomes *"life"* and the very reason to live. The idea of longing-for or nostalgic-for doesn't capture the emptiness of these days. I have friendships in Europe, Asia and the States that are dying because of absence. I cannot keep in touch. I'm out of touch.

Such an absence carries the kind of sadness that gives birth to ideas, ideas to fill such absence. Ones that come fruitfully to mind in my absence concern the loss of living because of an extraordinarily potent, transmissible and fatal version of the flu. We're not supposed to say that. We're supposed to suppress the very word "flu," even though it has as much in common with it as out of common with it. It is indeed a terrible flu that has taken millions of lives and is causing incredible suffering for individuals and their families. But it is also one that is the most data-driven in history, with the dual structures of science and corporate-owned media streaming information to terrify us into submission. We submit our bodies to perhaps the grandest science-media-government experiment of all time. In this experiment, we all see the data and we all are the test subjects. Submission to the experiment brings the promise of tiny openings (you get to remove your mask—a stupid reward); non-submission to the experiment brings shame (the rational get to shame the irrational). No one is forced, that's not how power works anymore. Instead, *choice* is socially coerced by being bound to the rational and the verifiable. This marks the atheist version of virtue against sin: rationalism over the irrational. Salvation comes in the preservation of the body rather than the soul.

There are always multiple truths to any namable event, and these are not in opposition or contradiction: 1) there is a highly infectious, mutating virus of biology, killing bodies and making a lot of people sick; 2) there is a highly infectious, mutating virus of thought, conditioning our minds for current and future submission and compliance; 3) there is a highly infectious, mutating virus of spirit, a sickness of psyche, turning the active into the passive, the joyous into the fearful, the expressive into the anxious.

Mind/thought/spirit: we are at last in tune with the planet, with our burning global ecosystem. It should never be forgotten that these viruses arise largely as a result of economic and technological progress—livestock production by multinational corporations, effective transportation of foods, and better tools and methods of mass deforestation. The continuance of this progress will produce a whole new generation of viruses, which we'll need more technology and more injections to resist. This is also a sickness, the sickness of the self—how we practice, how we eat, how we conform, how we comply, how we submit. We are, all of us, sick.

22 July, Kaohsiung

Here's a drinking game: Take a shot every time you see or hear the word "misinformation." On liquor sales alone, we'll save the global economic network for all eternity. It is The Word of 2021.

This is a sensitive issue, and it's become extremely taboo now —at the risk of silencing—to say anything outside of the singular, unified message of the State-media-science alliance. *Metoo,* an overdue and necessary rebellion against toxic masculinity and violence, has the consequence of conditioning us to control our language. It has readied us for this language of pandemic correctness, which is getting really creepy. We've shifted so much over the past year and a half that today I don't know if posting aberrant thoughts on social media will get me into some kind of trouble.

Adding to the creepiness is that in all of this screened living, I don't know if I'm living on some thought-island because I don't see anyone expressing the concerns I have over social media spaces. I do live on a literal island, and I don't spend much time with other people because my longtime friends and family live elsewhere. What I see as political activism and opinion is screened and performed. I don't know any alt-right assholes, so I don't know what they're saying. Unlike so many in the States, I'm safe from the random MAGA hat meatheads at the local Walgreens. I'm pretty much vaccinated against all that.

What I see is a lot of liberal shaming, like a *lot* of shaming, usually in joke form, coupled with buckets full of virtue signaling and puritanical posturing. This is doing real damage to my existing impressions of liberal grace, kindness and creative thinking. All this absence has been infecting my mind, slowly changing my mind, turning my mind into something different. My thirst for radical thought is radicalizing me.

My catharsis and my chorus are gone. It feels like only a short time ago I was communing in person with fellow philosophers gathered in Berlin or Singapore, sharing radical thoughts to push our horizons. We used to be able to gather in person, in public, in spitting range, and explode in viral ideas. From my screen, I don't see any fringe or outlier ideas expressed, except maybe a couple of people from my PhD program. I feel removed from the joyful rebellion of those days before 2019, a time which feels so far in the past. Maybe it's just my knowledge streams, maybe people are not as they appear. Everything now seeks approval.

Arendt writes about this, the analogue version anyway: the isolation that leads down paths of narrow and dangerous thought. Perhaps I too am trending toward the myopia I find so harmful. But I don't think so. I'm retaining my sense of spirit. I'm holding on to an ethics of the radical idea and the joys of creative uncertainty. The danger is in deciding, and everyone seems to have decided.

I cannot shake the idea that media *is the problem*, not a mirror of the problem. It is, to bring McLuhan and Husserl up to date, the lifeworld of thought and action. In the 1990s and 2000s, when technology was still promising, we called such a critique "technological determinism." I think it's safe to say that technology is on par with a viral condition. It is not so much *determining* thought and action, but it determines the narrow *range and means* of thought and action. Technology is not the top-down robotic master feared in the 1950s. Rather it is the architecture of the whole mechanism of thinking as a possibility. Technology is structuring opinion and belief through personal preferences. This is different from determining. It's not the house but rather the blueprint for building one's own thought. The structures of technology at their most effective pull openness into the cold narrowness of binaries and approvals.

Media and technology is a liberal development, liberal here in the sense of a once open field of experimentation (1990-2000 or so) in the development of digital communication. It soon became wrapped into the capitalist machine. Tech writers and culture writers overlapped into a Gen X futurism anxious to move away from the fixed technologies and attitudes of the past. They took over the conventions of network TV and came to own the messages that could be individually streamed into the liberal mind. Bringing this up to today, these attitudes have ballooned and the technologies have woken up a division between the contented and the discontented. The difference today is that the early utopianism is gone because it's no longer just a playground for liberal progress; now everyone can play. Conservatism, even hate, can push agendas into the future as well. They build from the same blueprint.

But the control of media remains dominated by this corporate-liberal (neoliberal) alliance with futurism, science and reason. This is great for centrist liberals and academics. The problem is that it seems to now be a mandate. It has lost the playfulness of the Gen X youth and has become spiteful. The moral thought of today's liberal rationalist is of the digital public good, but the strategies are becoming horribly resentful and divisive. Media writers today seem absolutely flummoxed that not everyone conforms to the dominant groupthink. This is making everyone, particularly these rationalists, insane. Reporters and content providers spend a lot of time Zooming with Very Important People talking about Very Important Things. In the midst of this stream, it's difficult to imagine—or care about—mental pathways other than these pathways that they traverse. In everyday conversation, real humans display a variety of thoughts and nuance. But any *screened* discourse narrows to this mediated language of performance. Since we're separated from each other more and more by screens, we live more and more of our lives *thinking* such language. With all this screened isolation, our minds are literally changing. Everything is archived, nothing can be forgotten or undone. Our minds think and express the morality of the platform.

Today's manifestation of this is the endless "misinformation" repetition. Who gets to decide what is information and what is "mis"? The Trump regime dead, it is the now benevolent regime—which is really an anti-Trump regime—directing what is missed in any information. It is a reaction to the malevolent administration, a new decree of determining "mis." In this version, we see emboldened writers unashamedly using "police" as a verb to arrest thought; we see a push to cajole a platform originally designed by a lonely weirdo to pick up chicks to monitor and report data on public opinion; we have people in charge of "content policy," when the content is people's opinions and beliefs. One of my social media horror-fascinations of late is to read the comments section of an NPR story on FB. It's filled with the most hateful human beings you'll ever come across. People who unashamedly wish for "others" (the unvaccinated) to die, people who celebrate mandates and identifications, people screaming for a kind of social Darwinism to take care of the deplorables. All of it aims to preserve the survival of the anti-Trumpist consciousness that has possessed liberalism.

In this advanced state of liberalism contra-Trump, Information is becoming the new object of devotion to replace Spirit. It is the vast, immanent material of faith to which we pray—the unquestionable, *transcendental* truth. Corporate media is the Church, through which priests (experts) channel the almighty *Logos*, speaking on behalf of God the State. "Misinformation" is a sin against material Information. The Devil coerces people into sin, spreading misinformation. Punishment of misinformation keeps our souls pure.

In Christian societies, the idea of eternal salvation was sold to preserve the Church-State alliance. In a Science society like today, the idea of preserving the earthly body is sold to serve the interests of the eternal economy. This God is an immanent one; it is not outside but within our souls and within our power to change if we find the courage to do so.

But I don't know how to do that. I believe, as almost everyone does, that I'm on the side of good. I don't know what the hell is going on with anti-vaxers and the far right; I have no interest or sway with them so I don't engage with them. Liberals are my people; they, we, are the ones I'm concerned about. What are our strategies? What's our joyful contribution? What are we fostering? I'm looking for some kind of light and heat, some non-reactionary ethics of goodness that I can get behind. Good to me is freedom of thought, tolerance to our brothers and sisters with different beliefs, a wide open public sphere of ideas, radical thinking, radical skepticism, and the joyous exchange of differences.

A truly ethical futurism would be one that remembers all those *Star Trek* episodes, which constantly remind us that once you achieve consensus in the idea, the panacea that seems too convenient, authority draws power from it, almost always with harmful results to individuals. Or remember George W. Bush—the danger of "with us or against us." This is now the cry of liberalism, which demands *allegiance* as free expression withers. The radicals have all fled, been pushed to the right with their crazy ideas that have become hateful through the resentment of being left out; or they've shifted further to the left, Antifa and the like. But the narrative of the left produces no interest to capitalist media except to shame it. Their discourse evaporated when the Democratic Party machine defeated Bernie Sanders. The truly frightening political situation is that the *right* are the organized rebels, the instigators and outliers defying the mandate as an expression of resistance against control and conformity. Meanwhile the liberal center takes on the mantle of dogmatic conservatism, casting mediated prayers to Information.

How did liberalism find itself here? And what do we want? Vaccines provide an interesting mirror here. Will we be satisfied with seventy percent conformity, eighty-five percent? Will we stop there or will we continue the self-justified sport of ridiculing those on the outside? Will a vaccine become the visible mark of virtue to the

Church of New Liberalism? Will we only be satisfied with total (self) control? These to me are vitally important questions. We're *making the world we think* right now.

We cannot forget Arendt's warning: Totalitarianism begins in isolation, is justified by logic, and dominates through a total accumulation of power. We've nurtured the architecture of the first, are now mandating the second, and are awaiting the emergence of the third. And everyone is participating.

26 July, Kaohsiung

Misinformation isn't the problem. Information is.

Every person with the disposable income to buy an internet-capable device can gather data, facts, reports, opinions, arguments, stories, images, sounds and words. In digital form, this is all information.

But let's presume for a moment that there is such a thing as "mis." What is it? Is it that something is missing? Yes and no. With information there is always plentitude, always *everything*; but this also means that something is always left out, even in mis-free information. Instead, the word signifies "wrong information." But we are all gathering information that is less than right. All information is directed; it has a directive. This is what we find in the Nietzschean-Foucauldain critique of truth as power. Information, as new power, is driven by something other than informing. The driving force is normally a profit motive. This can come through an individual or a multinational media corporation. At the individual level, we have a whole new breed of snake oil salesmen. At the mass level, the overwhelming majority of news information is funded by businesses seeking profits. In both cases, we have authority figures promoting an agenda. Can the "public good" be a virtuous agenda? Yes. But no virtue is pure; it cannot manifest as some universal perfection of mis-free information. News is not science, and even if it were it would still be about information over virtue.

Willful attempts at de-legitimizing scientific conclusions are harmful because they also have an agenda. This is legislated publicly through the verb "to misinform." But the more accurate signifier for this behavior is "to disinform." Usually *disinformation* is defined as willful, while misinformation is accidental. But *misinformation* has assumed the mantle of signifying nefarious intent. Perhaps then there is space here to consider a creative ethics of disinforming. If mis is *mis-take*, to give information in a way so that the take is intentionally missed, this is, again, harmful. To disinform would be to actively set aside information or to separate thought *from* information, to clean the mind of information, not necessarily as negation but as a clearing —to let something other than information flow into consciousness. Dis-*informing* oneself through distance—dis-*abling* one's *stance* from information—is good for the development of criticism. It would also encourage a reduction in conspiracies, which are built on information.

In all such terms, information itself remains the problem. To inform is to indoctrinate the *form*, the structure of "knowledge" as capital. We might think of it as in-knowing a form. In-*formation* as the *installation of form* cannot be the ethics. Information itself, as we're finding, is harmful and divisive. That's its function today as a force that accumulates power—to ossify thought into manageable (and profitable) identities. While we believe we can also individually gather such force into communal power, information is not built this way. It is built for machines of oppression and control, not liberation. A panopticon ethics will never make us free.

The philosophical tradition has shown repeatedly that virtue arises in the overcoming of common belief, of *doxa*. *Doxa* is the form, the in-*forming*, of belief and opinion. Information is today's *doxa*—the dominant and common belief at the level of society. *Doxa* is the social order, which means that information is the social order of our time. Information manages and sustains prevailing belief. Information is not truth, it is taught and learned. *Doxa*, doctra, doctor, doctrine, indoctrinate—an *in-doxination*. *Doxa creates* truth. *Doxa* is not manageable; it lies deep in the soul. It is internalized through the struggles over the power of ideas.

Plato's virtue is, again, a means of overcoming *doxa*. But Plato is wrong in today's age. His *epistemē* (scientific knowledge) cannot overcome *doxa*. Instead *episteme is doxa*.

What we need instead is a nurturing of *techne* and *poiesis* that breaks out of the *doxa* of information. An ethics of our age would be one of overcoming the general structure of information (as *doxa*), which includes the particular attempts to, as we say, misinform. To only do the latter, while ignoring the larger problem, is to prepare ourselves for a new totalitarian era beholden to information and its control.

Our problem is that the believers in the *doxa* of information do not practice skepticism; only the misinformed seem to be challenging *doxa*. What we need is to stop allowing ourselves to be informed or misinformed. We need to disinform ourselves—not totally, but through alternative and fluid techniques and practices. We need to create more strategies to upset the entire *doxa* of information that enables misinformation. Rather than policing misinformation, we need a creative dis-informing.

8 August, Seoul

"We are not awaiting either a new god or a new human being. We rather seek, here and now, among the ruins around us, a humbler, simpler form of life. We know that such a life is not a mirage, because we have memories and experiences of it—even if, inside and outside of ourselves, opposing forces are always pushing it back into oblivion."

- Giorgio Agamben[50]

I've been gravitating toward Agamben's concepts of "bare life" and "state of exception" more and more as this pandemic wears on. First, because these concepts fit well with what I seem to be developing lately, that of life over survival, or better stated, living over surviving. Second, because he's the only one I can find who has the courage to think critically through the emerging mandates of State control. There are of course other skeptics out there, but the vast majority are, at best, hiding behind some other agenda and/or, at worst, nutcases and fear peddlers. Agamben is not.

I just finished his recent book (released this May) *Where Are We Now?: The Epidemic as Politics*. It's a series of brief essays and interviews rendered between February and November, 2020, the period of time in which liberal democracies changed forever.

There is a lot to his writing that I disagree with, particularly his dismissal of the very real situation we find ourselves in. For example, he torpedoes his arguments with his frequent use of the qualifier "so-called" for very real things, such as, well, the pandemic. He claims that the "epidemic" was an "invention" (Ch 1). He makes

---

[50] All quoted material here is from the text: *Where Are We Now?: The Epidemic as Politics* (2021, ERIS).

assertions like these without argument or evidence, which brings him dangerously close to conspiracy type language. In an essay titled "Two Notorious Terms," he mentions The Bill and Melinda Gates Foundation, the WHO and something called "Event 201" without stating what this event is or making it clear what the causal connection is to the virus. He instead vaguely discusses "illicit objectives," but without elucidation or research that might allow us to investigate the connection. In a chapter about discreditations and conspiracies, he writes in the most irresponsible manner about both. He also appeals to hyperbole in comparing the current tactics of State control as worse than Fascism in Nazi Germany. I don't know, maybe at the level of methods implemented he is factually correct, but the association we have of those atrocities makes it feel like an overreach that dilutes the power of his more salient critiques of our current situation.

I don't mean to discount these problems in the book, but I am able to set them aside to read the other book that has also been written here. Agamben is not a research scientist or a journalist. He is doing philosophy, which means working through ideas and concepts to give us different ways of thinking through a political and philosophical problem. At this level, he succeeds. Through his writing, we can take a biological emergency and unwrap the dangerous political and discursive precedents being set by our collective acceptance right now. The value of this book is not to inform a reader about what was or what is; it is best read as a needed provocation as we dismantle and rebuild the structures of civic life. This is what political philosophy is best at—giving us a language to discuss collective action born of threats to freedom.

"Bare life" and "state of exception" are concepts Agamben has been working on the entirety of his philosophical career. To be overly simplistic, bare life is the reduction of an individual in society to a purely biological being, while a state of exception is the State's overreach to a crisis, one promised as temporary to deal with the crisis but which never leaves once implemented. Functioning together, these situations strip away the political potency of an individual, rendering collective society as docile. Exceptions are always offered in the best interests of the State *and* the individual, but end up advancing State control against individual and collective will. As he writes, "the state of exception is the mechanism by which democracies can transform themselves into totalitarian states" (Ch 9). Bare life, meanwhile, divides "the unity of our vital experience" into a "biological entity" on the one hand and a cultural and social existence on the other, then emphasizes the survival of the former at the expense of the latter. We see this lived out in the news media and through experts who demand biological survival at all costs, including (and this is what shocks Agamben) the needs of capitalism. Faith in the Science State has become so extreme as to even upset the powers of the Capitalist State.

Agamben is not simply intuiting these concepts; his work over three-plus decades traces the historical manifestations of such power, whether that is through the Church, the State, capitalism, science, or some combination. This makes the Covid age a timely one for Agamben's thought, and makes him well educated to discuss it. The combination he sees functioning with this current state of exception is one of medicine, digital technology and State control. The apparatus, as presented in the forward to the book, is "biosecurity." The aim of biosecurity is survival and control brought about through mediated consensus and conformity.

It is difficult to summarize the wealth of historical (genealogical) complexity Agamben is mapping out, but I'll try: Science is the religion of our time (Chs 5, 12). But more specifically, medical science is allied with State interests into a new "'Security State'" offering "medicine-as-religion." But unlike monks who gather in monasteries to pray together, this new religion isolates individuals from each other toward mere earthly survival (Ch 12). Agamben borrows from Foucault's notion of "biopower" to advance the idea of "biosecurity," which may seem like a sensible measure. But, he warns that in the hands of the State, "health... ceases to concern itself first and foremost with the agency of each individual and becomes, instead, an obligation which must at any cost, no matter how high, be fulfilled" (Ch 17). In other words, the only obligation is to survive. Yet within this, nothing has changed to encourage healthier diets and lifestyles; instead news media promotes faith in medical religion to save the body against the evil influence of disease. Science, through the State-media alliance becomes less about the scientific method and takes on cultish tendencies through experts (Ch 12).

> "If we look at the state of exception which we are now experiencing, we could say that the medical religion combines the perpetual crisis of capitalism with the Christian idea of the end times, of an eschaton where the extreme decision is constantly ongoing and where the end is simultaneously rushed and deferred in an incessant effort to govern it, without its ever being resolved."

We are well conditioned for exceptions to our freedom; it is central to our recent history (Ch. 6).

> "People are so used to living in conditions of perpetual crisis, that they seem not to realise that their lives have been reduced to a purely biological condition that has lost not only its political dimension, but also that of what is simply human. A society that exists in a perennial state of emergency cannot be free. We live in a society that has sacrificed freedom for so-called 'security reasons' and has hence condemned itself to living in a perpetual state of fear and insecurity."

With the virus, "bare life" has achieved its apex; the only concern is survival. Bare life has no means of unifying people together into an actionable community; instead it only encourages blindness and separation. The very term "social distancing" describes a political impotence, since action can only come in a crowd, through physical togetherness. The crowd, Agamben writes, overcomes the fear brought through isolation and paralyzation (Ch 7). The face, meanwhile, "is the site of politics" (Ch 19). In times when we are allowed to be together, we mask, which hides the expressiveness necessary for political action. When the pandemic is over, will distancing become the new "organizing principle" for future exceptions (Ch 8)?

The central problem is a singular ideological mindset on a global scale. The problem of ideology is always that it "makes sense" to society. The danger of this response to the virus, therefore, is that the solutions have already achieved global consensus. There are echoes of Orwell here, in how states of future totalitarianism, as depicted in *1984*, all utilize the same logical methods against their citizens, even as they go to war with each other. This is the universality of logic and reason that philosophy fights against, due to its dangerous conclusions. Without variations in thought and action, control is inevitable.

There is no question in my mind that Agamben is right in questioning this new valuation of survival over living. It's interesting for me to read this now, as I realize just how much this issue harmonizes with my own concerns over the future of life, freedom and artistic openness. Society has chosen survival, which is both expected and unfortunate in our time of biological fear. We need to find ways of breaking this, of challenging State control, while also imagining innovative ways of keeping the vulnerable safe, so that we can go back to living, instead of merely surviving.

The *future* question is equally challenging. A question that should be asked is what kind of track record Agamben has in his warnings about the future. For example, we need not ask whether 9/11 was a watershed event. It was. The question instead is did the *response to it* produce an ongoing state of control as normal? We still don't know the full answer because in a historical sense, the infrastructure of control as a response is still being actualized. Most of the Patriot Act was eventually neutered, and it has officially expired, which would seem to work against Agamben's argument of permanence. But we have collectively harbored its spirit *in ourselves*: increased wiretapping and surveillance with cameras everywhere (something we don't really notice any more); widespread tracking through mobile devices that we choose to carry (and with Covid, they have become necessities rather than a choice). We have drones above our heads that could be launched with impunity; we hear a passionate mandate-acceptance attitude nurtured by the necessity of near-universal vaccination. The list of 9/11-inspired security acceptance is a long one.

The state of exception that is Covid, to Agamben's point, has built upon this infrastructural change, fusing post-9/11 security with viral biology. Our practical acceptance of control technologies and State mandates for current needs and fears are troubling enough. But the more salient problem is in how they instill a habitual acceptance on the collective psyche for future exceptions. We are bound to see more limitations to human freedom, less tolerance of uncertainty, tighter restrictions on what may and may not be expressed. American liberalism is already deciding that anything outside of the Biden-science-technology discourse is to be scorned on social media. We have accepted the censorship of radical ideas. Scientists are now mouthpieces of State interests. Etcetera.

On these grounds, there is much to be concerned about. The current liberal discourse regarding Covid is to disparage the idiots who are fellow citizens in favor of the Democratic Party State that is currently in power. Doubt and skepticism are outright ridiculed. This change has happened at an incredible pace. Social media self-censorship and correction that began with the best of intentions (*#metoo*) set the standard for a regime of permissible language regarding the correctness of the Biden-science alliance. It's hard to fully grasp how much we've allowed censorship in only the last year. It bears repeating: Totalitarianism always thrives under the most rational and logical of intentions. Its tool of acceleration is the control of language.

Despite the book's problems, this is a hugely valuable, thought-provoking read, whether or not you agree. If one can set aside Agamben's rhetorical failings, the warning is one that should be considered before we willingly allow ourselves to sink into the loss of living for the sake of survival.

17 August, Seoul

What then is reason? How is it different from rationalism? These words have become highly technical and categorical over the course of intellectual history. My interest is not so much what reason is, but how the term is employed, and further, how it became so weaponized in political discussion. To borrow from Heidegger, what are we *calling* "reason"?

When someone throws out "reason," is the person advocating something Aristotelian, imploring someone's eudaemonic soul toward manifesting the good life? No. It's instead become a catch-all term (meaning: one that requires little thought) used to weaponize the superiority of one's own truth. "Reason" in this sense is used as an attempt to prove what is already an unassailable point. The word itself implies that the other is categorically anti-reason or using non-rational arguments. Reason in this reactionary way is employed to advocate against the messy human uncertainties of sensory living and undisciplined beliefs and opinions that give rise to what the self-proclaimed rationalist views as irrational thinking, usually some irrational faith. Reason by this definition describes an exercise of rationalizing the virtue of reason.

Reason, as a philosophical term, is different from this exercise of rationalizing. Early in philosophy, reason was connected with what is prior. There is a divinity to reason, and reasoning is a method of achieving what is fixed and already there in all persons. Reason commonly resides in God, in conformity to divine substance. I suspect people are employing the word in a post-Cartesian sense: a conformity to a logic, or at least a discipline of logical thinking, used to overcome doubts and faulty beliefs regarding the external world. But no one has the discipline of Descartes, sitting in bed and rigorously going through the process of stripping away all that can be doubted, in order to narrow existence to God and mind. Instead, we spend our time on websites scanning for rational ammunition.

Reason and rationalism are sometimes allied with science, and in some situations become synonymous. In this, it becomes something like what Jurgen Habermas called "cognitive-instrumental" reason—observation, prediction and hypothesis. This is then practiced as a "moral-practical" reason, becoming a political *rationalizing*. As far as I understand Habermas' argument, these two are in tension with each other. But in the weaponizing of reason, it seems we, the 2021 public, are employing instrumental reason as morality. This establishes the supremacy of reason as a weapon to target religious faith, regarded as anti-rationalist, to achieve a preconceived communicative goal. But again, if reason is prior, if it marks the innate greatness of human nature over that of the animal, it has little to do with science. Science is *empirical*; it studies the phenomena of nature and its various mechanisms and operations, including thought and consciousness. Reason comes from the inside, science approaches from the outside. They work well as particular disciplines to achieve prior aims, but they are not synonymous.

What I think is underway as a kind of zeitgeist involves a habituation of the lingering European tradition of arguing concepts of truth: one born of faith and one of reason. We have been well trained in the West to think in dualities of opposition, that two ideas are mutually exclusive. In a faith versus reason argument, the self-proclaimed rationalist and the self-proclaimed devotee to faith have no interest in changing what is prior as a concept of truth. The aim is instead rhetorical and performative. One is either an atheist and will argue reason against irrationality; or one is religious and will argue faith against any threat to it. Both arguments arise from a fixed, essential and unchanging belief in such essences.

What we forget, in a demand to adopt an essence of reason, is that most people are working through their *own* process of *reasoning*. Sometimes reasoning is rational process, other times something else. (Reasoning is a process; rational describes a method.) Thought is always in a process of becoming, working through an idea. This is something we all share: faith in one's inferences. One cannot force another person's thought process to align with one's own, unless that person wishes to force a society of Rational Authoritarianism, which I fear people tending toward in weaponizing an idea of reason. But remembering Socrates, one *can* change oneself and one's own thinking. This is the core tenet of philosophy. The best way to change one's outlook on any topic is, as Descartes rightly suggested, to think through all that one can doubt. God or a lack of God, both of which are essential beliefs, form the symbolic substance of certainty that extends to any, say political, argument. This is how argument emerges as dogmatic. What is needed is a willingness toward doubt and an acceptance that belief is always more vivid to the imagination than facts are.

Contra Cartesian rationalism, sitting still is not enough. The other needed ingredient that helps to overcome these essential oppositions is to have more real, lived experiences. Experiences give vitality to any reasoning process. Coupled with critical, skeptical and imaginative introspection, a variety of experiences broadens one's outlook on everything. Experience is also the experience of others, either in a community or in a new environment with people different from oneself. Experiencing the lives of others requires us to move *outside*, to be together with others. We find this severely restricted in a pandemic world of biological survival. The more we train people to become immobile, to *receive* information, to receive experience, the more we see a conformity to what someone else (some authority, for example) determines as, say, "rational" or "logical." Being sedentary and exclusively receptive turns rationalism into a material (rather than simply discursive) weapon. Experience, living, is the most vital means of overcoming the authority of imposed reason *and* dogma— achieving a demilitarization of such essences.

18 August, Seoul

Doing a second reading of Freud's Civilization and Its Discontents, *hovering in thought after Section III...*

Individual happiness is the aim of life. Two goals drive this striving: absence of pain and feelings of pleasure. But only pleasure is what we name as happiness. Freud's famous "pleasure principle" determines the purpose of life, "yet its programme is at odds with the whole world" because it is "incapable of being realized; all the institutions of the universe are opposed to it."[51] Freud reads a little like Schopenhauer or Kierkegaard (without mentioning them) here in writing that happiness only comes suddenly, while unhappiness is easier and more ongoing. Absence of pain (suffering) is more complicated. It's the self-tempering of one's individual happiness for

---

[51] Referencing here, and all quotes that follow, the David McLintock translation (2002, Penguin Books).

the modest needs of the "'reality principle'," which pushes happiness into the background. In other words, we give up happiness so we may escape unhappiness.

Civilization drives this tempering for the sake of the community. Its concern is one of rights over individual brute force and the external power of justice. "Individual liberty is not an asset of civilization." Civilization carries much of the blame for our suffering and misery, so we are hostile to it. We feel discontent toward civilization when confronting how institutions and technology have de-natured us. We imagine that perhaps times were better with less of it.

What comes to my mind (this is not Freud) is how community functions smoothly when it 1) maintains an ethics of *individual* liberty, of living and expressing; and 2) is not compromised by a *collective* subjugation of living and expressing. The burden of the health of the communal psyche should not fall on the individual as the object of condemnation; nor should our solution be a subservience to the powers of the State. We should be able to collectively recognize when the state has overreached its power against all individuals, without transferring blame to the individual. The problem is how civilization (the society), not the individual, fails the community. In other words, the problem is less about the threat of "stupid people," and rather the psychic health of civil society. This opens the question: What kind of community is liberalism encouraging? Or put another way, what kind of community does liberalism want to build?

Mandates, shaming, surveillance, control, absurd wealth inequality, etc. are all aspects of the liberal agenda in 2021. Together, it pushes the "happiness" drive to a limit it cannot contain, not without the mass collective psychosis or/and violence we are witnessing. Liberalism has become driven by wealth and technological pragmatism; it simultaneously deflects blame by ascribing cause to the imagined individual transgression so it may preserve its own power. Liberalism today is society overwhelmingly burdened by civil power. Mediated social discourses—enacted by individuals and corporate news entities—encourage and maintain this power through mediated participation and consumption.

This draws me back to the concept of resentment (Nietzsche's *ressentiment*), which I believe is the driving force of Trump-Covid politics. *Ressentiment* and bad faith have their roots in Christianity. Contemporary atheism has internalized the juridicial, transcendental law of Christianity into its morality. Resentment today is not exclusive to any political party, but is all-encompassing. Hatred has not *possessed* conservatism like some evil demon. Nor is liberalism the angel that saves us, as it too resents, reacts, and assigns blame. Hatred and resentment come when one feels overpowered by an attitude and an ideology that an individual is powerless to overcome. As Deleuze writes about Nietzsche's concept, *ressentiment* fills the gap; it expresses itself as a negative power, producing a "reactive triumph" and "an imaginary revenge."[52] Hate comes from a feeling of powerless reactivity, of a need to negate the object of an encroaching master that one takes as the threat. Since liberalism continually shifts the target of such a master, the resentment attacks anyone symbolically attached to that master: say, Biden, black and brown people, women, vaccines, etc. It's a revolt of the psyche, not of any political allegiance. The political party (in this case opportunistic Republican politicians) or hate groups, for example, simply arrange the forces of resentment using language that promises "the triumph of the weak *as* weak... slaves *as* slaves."

An individual must carry responsibility for hatred and engaging in hateful acts. But resentment is also a collective problem not exclusive to any side. This is what centrists and progressives fail

---

[52] Here, and Deleuze quotes that follow in this entry: Gilles Deleuze, *Nietzsche and Philosophy* (1983, Athlone Press).

to recognize. The psyche isn't about party, it's rather that party becomes the Freudian father/authority to rally around. Resentment in a lifeworld of digital, fragmented information happens at the subjective, existential level. A Biden voter can feel the slave entrapment just as easily and express a different resentment. Here, we can consider what Deleuze calls the resentful atheist—"the European Man," the reactive atheist who killed God. There is no side in Nietzsche, Freud and Deleuze; there are conditions of the psyche as a collective condition that draws people into aligning with a side, a side that is culturally and socially mediated into divisions. The psyche of resentment always shapes itself as dialectical—the identification of evil that responds "I am good." It reacts and opposes.

Reactiveness to medical science comes *because it is mandated,* because the communal body is legislated as more important than the individual body. To mandate a vaccine that came upon us very fast expects that an individual give her/his own body over to the body of liberalism and the collective interests of society. Liberalist ideology becomes the God of the State against the God of Nature and Heaven. The vaccine is political *because* the politics of liberalism demands a conversion of greater finality than that of the psyche—it demands the handing over of one's *body.* It marks a total conversion of one's system of beliefs to another, that of liberal power. To suggest that the vaccine is political fails to recognize the full scope. For many, the vaccine is a total religious conversion.

The problem, however, is not just in this opposition. Liberalism has failed *itself* by thoroughly discounting those members that make up the most vital element of its congregation. From the election of Trump through the lingering reality of the pandemic, liberalism has marginalized its artists, rebels and progressives for the needs of centrist conformity. A strident emphasis on correctness, rationalism and survival is antithetical to art and action. Survival leads to lockdown mentalities as a general state-mandated *morality.* Activists, the instigators of change, are restricted in their need to gather, antagonize, shout, express. The situation is even worse for artists, the producers of beauty and ideas, who thrive on the vigor of chaos against the demands of centrist conformity. They are being denied their need to play, sing, shout, perform, express.

The activist gathering still has its element of improvisation and publicity. With disobedience at its core, it maintains its possibility. But artists who perform *require* the agreement of society's laws to make their art for the public. Yet both aspects—as well as the progressive drive toward more radical solutions to the immanent dangers of ecological disaster and the continued problem of wealth disparity—share in a feeling of being left out by one's own people.

Another element to this that cannot be ignored is that these fringe aspects of liberalism consist largely of young people and people in child-free unions. They have more will and incentive to live rather than just survive. Centrists largely consist of skittish Democrat-voting parents who, for valid reasons, panic over their children's futures. The pandemic, vaccine mandates, lockdowns and other State mandates of survival, are easy to accept for such survivalists. If these aspects of control increase, as travel, art and protest eviscerate, we'll see even more pressure for artists to fold into the traditional stasis of centrist ideologies such as staying at home and raising families.

Art will die, or at least be radically transformed into a socially acceptable mask for "art." Knowing this at an often instinctive or unconscious level, artists, activists, rebels and other true progressives still fighting to live are fleeing the centrist mandate. Whether some choose to rush to more libertarian elements of conservatism or choose to remain unaligned and outside of the political spectrum, is a question currently underway. Regardless, this centrist liberal power of survival has secured its alliance with science (the industries of health, technology and media) and abandoned the most productive instigators of new thought and ideas. Living is always far riskier than surviving.

This is why a critique of liberalism is the more vital discussion than a critique of conservatism. Liberalism is the master, the dominant power. It is pushing the agenda of human survival as an earthly salvation. If liberalism were to shift its *strategies* toward inclusion, courage and free expression, and reduce its techno-capitalist and neoliberal conformity as *policy*, I'm convinced that two things would result: 1) the "brute force" of individual extremism would mollify, and 2) a sense of inclusive community would return to liberalism, sparked by the return of artists, activists, radicals and free thinkers who once believed in the progressive drive toward better societies.

21 August, Seoul

Continuing my reading of Freud's Civilization and Its Discontents...

In Sections V-VIII, Freud introduces the driving force of aggression, moves to the death drive and its relation to Eros, and draws all of this into his concept of the super-ego as both internal and cultural.

The problem of civilization lies in the tension between the individual and the collective. Individual aggression (sexual, according to Freud) is the "original, autonomous disposition" against civilization.[53] Civilization's response lies in its capacity to draw this drive into the collective—marriage, law, love thy neighbor, etc. These civil unifications run "counter to basic human nature." Law, for example, "cannot deal with the subtler manifestations of human aggression." Every adult faces situations of abandoning the

---

[53] *Civilization and Its Discontents* (2002, Penguin Books).

community to return to the aggression of youth. This tension produces violence or, as curtailed, leads to misery, anxiety, loss of freedom and general unhappiness.

Freud's psychology is described through various drives. He begins Section VI with Schiller's concept of the world as held together by hunger (the self-preservation drive) and love (the species-preservation drive). Love for Freud becomes "Eros" while hunger becomes his "death drive." Civilization is in "service of Eros," gathering people into a "libidinal" bond we call "humanity." The tension between them explains "the phenomena of life." They are not separated, rather the death drive and its aim of aggression and destruction becomes "pressed into the service of Eros." They are "alloyed with one another" and become unrecognizable.

The super-ego is Freud's concept of a conscience—aggression is internalized *against* the ego's tendencies, as the ego takes on the norms of conscience. A sense of guilt is its driving factor. His concept of guilt is complex, but it's born of a former father/parent-figure authority replaced by the community. In short, fear/love of an authority figure becomes fear/love managed in a super-ego relation. The super-ego internalizes guilt brought on by the authority of the community against sinful behavior. This exchange weakens the individual, "setting up an internal authority to watch over him." It's interesting that for Freud, the more virtuous a person is, the more stern the authority and the greater the self-accusation of sin.

The super-ego is psychoanalyzed in the individual, but Freud here proposes a cultural super-ego. The feeling of guilt is expressed as "an unconscious need for punishment," which leads to unhappiness, malaise and anxiety. The individual ego cannot stop the drive toward happiness and pleasure, while the "cultural" process "is usually content with a restrictive role." Individual happiness is pitted against human fellowship.

The super-ego works at the unconscious level. When brought forward to consciousness, it collides with the cultural super-ego. Freud suggests that this is normal, producing a "cohesion" between the development of the mass and the individual. So, aspects of the super-ego can be recognized more through the community than the individual. The cultural super-ego produces its "demands" concerned with ethics. Ethics for Freud is a kind of therapy, reminding us of the merit of "compliance."

From here, Freud drops the idea of the cultural super-ego when one wishes—that is to say, *this* reader wishes—he would go further. Instead, he concludes the book by saying that this concept needs more study. Of interest to him is to wonder how civilization will manage the disturbances of life that continue with the human inclination for aggression and destruction.

What I wonder, what I continue in my own thinking, is this: If there is a super-ego acting at the individual unconscious level, can we not also attribute, at least conceptually, a *cultural unconscious* to the super-ego—that is, operating at the level of culture itself? As with the individual, the cultural super-ego remains unconscious, transcendental, and functioning smoothly in its continuity. But what happens when something triggers an emergence to the forefront of consciousness—say a global event of some kind? Freud was writing in the shadow of WWI, a distinctly exterior event of bullets, bombs, explosions and death. It is a conscious horror that intersects and ruptures the continuity of the unconscious.

How can this be drawn into a global pandemic psyche? This too is a real event in name, playing out as a plurality of multiple interconnecting events, but its conscious relation is interior and invisible. Its violence is a biological invasion and collapse of great uncertainty. Rather than bullets there are particles and droplets that come through laughter, a raised voice, a song, a cough, or a close exchange of words. The invisible threat may or may not house itself within the body. Perhaps one's droplets do violence to a body, perhaps not. This is a different collision of individual super-ego and cultural super-ego. It is a threat hard to see for its actual violence. But this is not only at the level of the virus. The solution, the reaction, the fight, is also invisible. The opposition is a shot inserted into the body by the kindly nurse who administers the invisible authority of medical science. We are not prepared for this kind of battle because we are trained to *see* our knowledge, to see our *knowing*. This violence remains largely unconscious and unseeable, which is something more practiced at the consciousness of *belief*. The pandemic, its vaccine, and the information surrounding them ignite a battle of biological and digital affectation whose speed far exceeds the rational mind's ability to gather and ascertain. For so many, individualism and its drives cannot conform to this culture that accepts restrictions and mandates against happiness. We progressives pray to a rational God, one who has absconded, who has no power here. The pandemic war is one of New Faith.

Freud wrote that as aggression becomes guilt, libidinal drives are converted into symptoms. We're seeing the symptoms playing out as a shared illness. What is shared is a drive to eliminate the other's unconscious. This epidemic of a pandemic so far has been an unconscious struggle of drives. The cultural super-ego of media proliferation—itself a virus that has not only infected but entirely possessed the cultural unconscious—has split people into two types. This threatens to destroy the variety of opinions, beliefs and understandings that are needed as a means of therapy.

Everyone who fights, gets angry, and feels anxious at the conscious level is someone who cares about happiness. This is what we share. The instinctual drive of happiness has come under threat by a perceived other as the object that threatens this goal. Unconsciously denied in this is the super-ego of liberal, civilized society that is falling apart. It's falling apart because our drives toward active joy have been stripped away in favor of the needs of civilization's survival. One cannot destroy civilization (the father), so one turns against the sibling. Each of us strives to destroy the aspect of the family unit that will not conform to the needs of the ego. We all, that is civilization itself, need therapy.

28 August, Busan

"Did my own research," "I trust my own immune system," "who stands to gain?," "free thinker," "taking my chances," etc... These used to be considered virtues of liberalism, the rational mind, the free spirit, the radical against the mandates of religion and State. Now we ridicule such people in simple-minded memes, and take resentful joy in the comments—"So irrational!" We love to dismiss people we feel are stupider than we are—*We Moralists* who have given our religious devotion to the State. It's terribly sad how we shame free thinking.

The concern is not this crisis, but how we are habituating minds of the future to grant unwavering religious devotion to the media-science-technology matrix. Liberalism has failed because we have become so fearful of the individual thought. So we pray, one meme at a time, to the immanent God of Reason, the almighty Father in the form of the moral State, the savior of all reasoned-kind.

30 August, Seoul

Two prominent philosophers I've tried to find value in and always fail: Hegel and Marx. They are gaping holes in my ability to think/write philosophically, particularly in regard to politics. Having studied "around them," for a decade, I feel like I know both already. It's as if I'm going to parties and they're always there. I lean in to conversations, I talk to people who have talked to them, and I've decided they're not speaking what sings to me. I'm not interested in an intimate relationship with either of them.

Nevertheless, here I am making another attempt, this time through Henri Lefebvre's *Hegel, Marx, Nietzsche: or, The Realm of Shadows*.[54] A third of the way through, I find myself confirming my biases. Hegel's and Marx's rigidity does little to address belief, process, even that so-Hegelian word "spirit," in a way that sings any melody that moves me. The dialectic, in both thinkers, is to me a mistake of history, composing the dominant mode of reactivity in social consciousness, an elevation of oppositions and negations, the failure of revolution as an actionable concept. But whenever Lefebvre moves to write on Nietzsche, the windows open, sunlight enters in streams, the prose sings; the psyche comes out to play, joy emerges in creative acts, value rises above structures and institutions; determinations of history, hierarchy and essence fade. Power becomes an active force. We're no longer being, we're living. *Überwindung*!

Lefebvre describes the "Nietzschean revolt" in a way that was not so shunned, even a year ago: "the stubborn defence of civilization against the pressures of society, state and morality." In Hegel and Marx, the rational and the real are the same, composed in a logico-dialectical identity and union of contradiction and struggle. For Nietzsche this is a mistake. "It rationally associates fact with value or meaning; but facts have no more meaning than a pebble on a mountain or an isolated noise." Nature has no meaning, only a "mixture with no name." People create meanings by naming things and evaluating them, and it's here that people get into trouble, becoming abstracted. What's needed instead is a "gay science," a

---

[54] Here, and all quotes that follow: 2020, Verso Books.

joyful science to save us from the Greco-Roman *logos* of logic and law and the Judeo-Christian moral puritanism that remains at the European heart.

From here Lefebvre dips into Augustine, and I found this section fascinating. Augustine (whom I've read, but not in this sense) proposed three libidos: the need to dominate, knowledge toward things, and the pursuit and failure of pleasure. This is mirrored in the Holy Trinity: the father (power, dominance), the Son (knowledge, *Logos*), and the Spirit (true love). The father and son are not enough, only spirit can save us. Lefebvre writes: "The Spirit is subversive or it is nothing. It is embodied in heretics, rebels, the pure who struggle against impurity. It brings with it revolt and joy. Only the spirit is life and light."

Nietzsche's gay science is not a rhetoric of love, but a spirit of living, a festival of body, art and poetry. With spirit:

> "Living and lived experience forcefully reassert themselves, with violence if need be. Against whom and against what? Against the coldest of cold monsters, the state. Against sad (conceptual) knowledge, against oppressive and repressive violence. Against the everyday, against unacceptable 'reality'. Against labour and the division of labour and the production of things. Against social morality and constraints, those of a society without civilization that seeks to perpetuate itself by any means."

Against Hegel and Marx, Lefebvre writes, this Nietzschean overcoming preserves nothing. It is not revolutionary but "subversive." This brings me back to the notion of *strategies*, which as sinologist philosopher François Jullien writes is the *alternate*, Eastern concept to Western concentrations on "being."[55] Liberalism fails at the level of strategies. It now aims to preserve the state at the expense of

---

[55] François Jullien, *From Being to Living* (2020, Sage).

the individual, the biological being at the expense of living in its becoming. Liberalism is a failure of discourses and methods, a failure to face death, to take chances, to risk living.

I buy Lefebvre's argument that these are the three principle thinkers of modernity (although I'd argue as well for Freud, whom he mentions, and Foucault). Two of them compose a problem; one is a way through to something brighter, more joyful, and more expressive. And for me, Deleuze picked up the best of Nietzsche, nested him with Spinoza and Bergson, and gave us an ethics of expression, action and generative potential that deserves even greater attention than it already gets in philosophy. Deleuze's synthesis leads the way to a potential "creative ethics" to overcome today's puritanical moralism that transposes Roman-Catholic methods into Atheist Liberal Techno-capitalism.

31 August, Seoul

It's interesting how we replace patterns of civilized, communal ethics with different signifieds. In 2016, the mandate was "voting." If you weren't voting you were the problem, even though the individual vote is mathematically insignificant. In 2021, the mandate is vaccination. If you aren't vaccinating you are the problem; in this case vaccination has tremendous individual significance. Yet, played out discursively, its anxiety factor is on par with the communal ethics of voting.

Both are un-*civilized* choices, that is, antagonistic to the civil community. What's different at the political level is that the vote mandate was levied against a member of one's own community. Today, the mandate is levied against the presumed other, who in reality is impossible to define. The air of accusation is the same while the specific reactions are different: To be uncivilized in 2016, you deserve to be unfriended. To be uncivilized in 2021, you deserve the death that will come to you.

There are other examples of such patterns: the virality of socially mediated information, with its Trumpist hate- and virtue-casting, all cultivating within the same infectious lifeworld, a kind of digital/psychological plague; the virology of bodies, with Trumpism now as a plague that continues to destroy biological life through the culpable bodies of anti-vaxers.

But also, we see the same patterns of resistance manifest through heretics. I suppose many of the "hesitant" also couldn't bring themselves to vote for HRC.

The political is now fully viral in every conceivable way. There's something distinctly Christian to all of it... God and Satan scattered into different names—Trump, Fauci, Reason, Science, Law, Fact. Viruses do not care about names. Through our bodies and thoughts, through our lifeworlds and ecosystems, they live.

CODA

1 September, Seoul

Where do we find ourselves, in September of 2021, as political souls functioning as members of highly developed societies?

We find ourselves submerged within the rising power of media and its capacity to overtake the psyche of the believing, active subject, rendering us anxious, reactive and resentful. This plays out at a highly conscious and rational level as a battle of "facts" versus "fake," but the problem is far deeper than such oppositions. News media, ostensibly engaged in the documentation of history for the public good, is an industry grounded on advertising revenue to meet the profit motive demanded by whichever corporation owns it. With social media, this illusion of institutional objectivity has transformed into an illusion of individual empowerment as free expression. The corporate trinity of expression (Twitter, Instagram, Facebook) is commodifying the individual in different, far more pernicious ways. As with the news media, these companies aim to centralize, occupy and mine thought. But they do so by tuning the *participatory*, rather than the previously *accepting*, psyche. At the same time, media technologies are dividing the self from the sensory world of physical, co-present experiences with others. They reduce rather than enable the possibility for political action as an instigator of lasting change.

The economic necessities of Covid-19 techno-capitalism are dividing us socially by replacing togetherness with mediated communication.

We find ourselves politically within a growing antagonism between the potential of the living, sensory self and the institutional power of the state-science-capitalist alliance ("the State"). Any functioning nation requires some variable balance of control, security and liberty; capitalism produces the wealth that maintains State legitimacy and power. This alliance has been flourishing for many nations, particularly since World War II. The third aspect of the union is science, an institution whose pure methods lead to great advancement, but whose entry into the state-capitalist alliance is bearing full fruit with the ongoing pandemic. Medicine and digital technology in particular are two areas of economics and government that are thriving at alarming levels. Adding to the trouble this brings is the fanatical devotion the rational majority has to the *idea* of science in mediated discourses. In this time of liberal atheist power, science has become the new Church. It is not the transcendent God-like authority of old. It is the pervasive, immanent, collective production of a new-and-improved authority that drives a logic of conformity and control. This is why the old models of power no longer speak to our time. This new power isn't State versus individual. It's not ideologically imposed from the top down. Instead, it functions inside out. Our consumerism and our belief in our mediated ideas of science (as church) through experts (as priests) produces this power. Our 2,000-year-old structural programming of *belief* has transitioned our psyches from one model to another. The dark underbelly of *liberalism* has revealed itself in the self-producing, state-science-capitalist alliance functioning today. The question for the future is: What world are we building through our cooperation with this new institutional alliance? What is our place, as living beings, in this future we are making?

We find ourselves in the midst of a significant uptake in laws, rules and regulations—some documented, others threatened, and many more unconsciously subsumed. We are very aware that our expressions and experiences are moderated more than ever by the State and by others acting on behalf of the State. We work for its interests through our citizenry, in how we watch each other and base our distant friendships and alliances on the quality of our information about each other. We make daily affirmations of approval and condemn appearances of perceived evil. We are the congregation, casting prayers in the name of the transcendental goodness of Law. We "like" so that we may forget, so that the psyche may survive.

We find ourselves in an era in which nothing in culture and society goes unnamed and unevaluated. To name is to generalize and identify, to turn a single expression into a general indictment. Naming doesn't begin a discussion, it's a means of ending it. The emergence of a pop critical-theory awareness produces an endless stream of diagnoses by name to eradicate the singularity of an expression. Our anxieties are pathologically driven. Digital culture encourages us to fetishize psychological and biological maladies: Identify a disease and shut it down, one person at a time, before it goes viral. Such diagnoses are made not by doctors or scientists but by social media influencers and their allies. This is the very condition of the liberalist tradition overlaid upon a viral time—a viral psychology from Trump to Covid. In 2016, we were determined to gather together and resist. In 2021, we have all become infected instead by a disease that is reactive, oppositional and negative. Liberalism has no positive ethics, at least none visible over media technology, the technology that marks the spirit of the time. Liberalism today isn't activism; it's entirely reactive to the disease of Trumpism.

We find ourselves lamenting the "loss of the humanities" while forgetting that the spirit of this idea requires the risk of dangerous art, of radical outlier thought and expressions. We situate this understanding, rationally, in a valuing of "art." We will say that art is always political, always residing at the level of ethics. But we have compartmentalized it, confined it to a safe liberal expression against illiberalism, a permissible approval of antitheses as reactions. Truly original art never reacts; it antagonizes, affirms and creates anew. But in an atmosphere of approval, we have turned against the radical, the dangerous, the otherwise. The liberal incorporation of art doesn't antagonize state control but functions to reinforce a conformity to liberalism alone. This is a citizen demand, under the thumb of Social rather than State rule. Art, *poiesis*, thereby falls under the rubrics of the capitalist-state-science alliance through the goodness of citizens. We, as citizens, no longer turn to art to express a radicalization of politics, ethics or aesthetics. We turn to the constructions of the capitalist State that we have integrated into ourselves. The State, as Freud diagnosed, is the caring but authoritative father to the confused and fearful child-citizen. Instead of practicing art—developing the slow perfection of a form of expression, a poetics, a technique—we work the language of the State that we ourselves have developed as a prophylactic against a disease of ignorance. Nothing is created in this inoculative, representational formula. Instead of making, we reproduce social laws and new, reactive norms. We look to experts, authority, truth and facts and copy graphs, evidence and text into social media feeds. We are not artists but reproducers of the sameness of others, a consensus built to pummel oblique minds into submission. It is the very worst kind of *mimesis*. We are no longer "against" the State, we are one side of the state of control against the other side of the state of control. This is what Trumpism gave birth to, which flourished during Covid: the antithesis that legitimizes the continuing power of the State. Bidenism doesn't exist. It's a reaction that upholds Trumpism through reactivity. We appeal to the correctness and righteousness of this other state of the State, and State control advances. It advances *through us*. We become the fortress that entraps us. Our language of reasonable experts and our condemnations of spirit, expression and radical thought, preserve the language and the legitimacy of State interests. The danger isn't in what this is now, but in what future forms this architecture will produce.

The core *idea* that emerged over the course of these writings is that of the virtue of living above the morality of survival. "Survival" preserves the body so that it lives (and shops, consumes, uses, votes, produces, etc.). "Living" is not preservation but instead being alive as a free spirit, living with other free spirits. At best, a balance of the two is established. But *survival* has become the sole liberalist *ethos*. To live, we need to call into question the demand for survival at the cost of living. This requires a critique of the strategies of mediated liberal discourse.

The core *critique* that emerged is that of "liberalism." It's a difficult word to contain since it has undergone such rapid transformation. In its broad and historical sense, it is not about a liberal-conservative (or Democrat versus Republican) divide; nor is it about "liberty," as that word is used politically today. Liberalism is a centuries-old idea and project that advances Enlightenment ideals of individualism, rationalism and science. It's a European idea that has been exported around the world. Traditionally, it emphasizes the power of the individual in relation to the State. In today's liberalism, however, the individual has transformed—through labor, science, technology, and education—into an acolyte of State interests. What I found myself criticizing is how this programming has infected the discourse and rhetorical strategies across the media streams we consume and speak through, as believers in the liberal idea. Dialogue has become intransigent in its adherences to the authority of rationalism and science against the expressiveness of skepticism, art and spirit. We cannot simply blame "illiberalism" as the problem. We must have the courage to inquire as to how liberalism came to this point. It has become consumed with the survival of *itself as an idea* at the expense of living expressions of creative uncertainty.

At this point in the text, I'm supposed to end, as most philosophical works of ethics do, with something positive to carry forward. After all, isn't this an ethics of joy? This is the hardest part of philosophy, the one that usually fails. But I will try.

To propose, briefly, such an ethics, it's important that a reader appreciate the value of non-binary and non-oppositional thinking. Liberalism is the power center, but it has no functional opposite. Conservatives and traditionalists also participate in upholding its power. At the same time, liberalism is a "liberal" creation and ongoing project, advanced mostly through center-liberal policies, attitudes and habits. The danger is that the "anti" to liberalism is chaos and creative unrest. Sadly, this field of play has been occupied by extremist tendencies, which use strategies of oppositional violence to reinforce identities. What we need is to bring the element of creativity, play, and free expression back to the side of joy—a multiplication of joy. "Joy," in this Nietzschean sense, is not happiness or positivity, it's the *poiesis* of creativity and newness. Joy is critical, interpretive, affirmational and constructive. The critique required is one of liberalism itself, a critique which opens to expressions outside of opposition.

Liberalism has manufactured a division between the liberal-centrist (the "rationalist") and the reactive-right (the "alt-right"). From this, strategies form, all of which are, in reality, reactive. The tactic of the alt-right advocate is to lie, or if that's too strong, to mislead. Lying and misleading are not areas conducive to philosophy. The tactic of the liberal-centrist is to produce a truth, not as an absolute but as an idea brought about through a process of belief. Truth is the field of philosophy. This is why liberalism needs to be put under the philosophical microscope. The *problem of liberalism* is that it is controlled by the liberal-centrist *ethos* of material and thought production (technologically, socially, economically, psychologically). Rather than opposed, this liberalism needs to be critiqued and analyzed from the inside out, at the level of psyche. The problem of the liberalist psyche is its increasing universalist tendency toward conformity and puritanism, and further, how it encourages the very problems of opposition we find today. What is required is an affirmation of *difference* instead of opposition. From this, survival—of bodies, identities, thoughts and ideas—gives way to the germination of new life and the potentiality of new living.

The joy that I feel is necessary is to break out of this inexorable viscosity of control and correction. Philosophy often speaks of "the rupture," the event that leads to change. From this can come a revolution in thinking. Revolution would have us attempt to reverse the stream of *virality* in the opposite direction. But virality doesn't work this way. Such a reversal is impossible and destructive. It's not how viruses work. We know full well that revolution is a failure: the use of power to oppose power, autonomy through unity and conflict... it's destroying us.

Healing can never come through the exertion of oppositional power. It can only come by encouraging a liberation in the power of *thinking differences* against identification. Care comes through what is close. To give people a reason to care about what is good in all of us, each of us needs some means of expression that affirms against, not in opposition to, the negative and reactive. The internet and its information utterly fail at nurturing this. It screens and divides, identifies and condemns. It produces distances of easy accusation. Hate abounds. We need expressions that bring us closer to each other in sensation, in community, in literal spitting distance of each other.

Information will go on as it does, manufacturing capital under the mask of freedom. We cannot turn back time, nor can we oppose it. But within the intense speed of information, one should find a way (and one should *encourage* others to find ways) to snap out of the main line—not to leave the world, but to mutate obliquely, vertically, *partially*, to take on a variable relationship with speed.

Sometimes the movement should be faster, other times very much slower. But it cannot oppose, it cannot be *reactionary*, it *must be other*.

    This is why creativity is so vital to a future that lives. *Mimesis* imitates, but true creativity is necessarily viral. It infects the psyche. Once we realize that the problem isn't of bad people but bad conditions of history and psyche that affect *everyone*, then we can open up to the production of active viral spreads. For this to happen, we need new viruses, new infections. We need the courage to destroy the bloated demands to conclude, which are weighing down the psyche. We can't inoculate our failures of the past; we can't inoculate ourselves from our fear of death; we can't inoculate ourselves from the ingrained opinions and beliefs of others that we now see vividly through the technology that liberalism produced and which we nurture. At this point, we can only draw forth the courage to risk the spread of something different. As Nietzsche suggested, we need to elevate *chance* as an active force against the incessant need to contain and control. If we can't, if there's no ledge to leap from, the whole leviathan will die a very boring death.

ABOUT THE AUTHOR

James studied philosophy at the European Graduate School with an emphasis on Deleuze, Bergson and Heidegger (Ph.D.); media and cultural studies at San Francisco State University with an emphasis on audiovisual aesthetics and technology (MA); and journalism and philosophy at San Jose State University (BS). His most recent book is *Terrence Malick's Unseeing Cinema* (Palgrave Macmillan, 2018). He teaches filmmaking and storytelling and lives with his wife in Seoul.

These fragments will continue to be authored and shared at jimbatcho.com/updates.